老城市

OLD CITY

OLD LHASA

A Sacred City at Dusk

Text by Ma Lihua

Text by: Ma Lihua
Photos by: China No. 2 Archives
Chen Zonglie
Translated by: Wang Mingjie
English text edited by: Yu Ling
Edited by: Lan Peijin

First edition 2003

Old Lhasa
A Sacred City at Dusk

ISBN 7-119-03124-4

© Foreign Languages Press
Published by Foreign Languages Press
24 Baiwanzhuang Road, Beijing 100037, China
Home Page: http://www.flp.com.cn
E-mail Addresses: info@flp.com.cn
sales@flp.com.cn

Printed in the People's Republic of China

OLD CITY SERIES

CONTENTS

Chapter 1 Lhasa at the Turn of the 20ᵗʰ Century

Chapter 2 Past Ages

Chapter 3 The Kaleidoscope of Barkor Street

The Potala Palace, widely regarded as the symbol of Lhasa, has been included in UNESCO'S World Cultural Heritage list. Photo* 1957.

* Photos marked with an asterisk were taken or provided by Mr. Chen Zonglie.

Chapter 1
Lhasa at the Turn of
the 20ᵗʰ Century

Lhasa and the Potala Palace in 1660, a reproduction made on the basis of a sketch by the Austrian Jesuit Johannes Gruber. The city wall in the picture was demolished by Qing Dynasty soldiers in 1720.

The bridges and waterways which used to be in front of the Potala, had been replaced by a large square.* (1950s)

Statue of Songtsan Gampo (c. 617-650), enshrined in the Potala. *

Lhasa's Turbulent Past

What is it that has enticed us to look back at the past of the city of Lhasa? What can we learn from those old sepia photographs? Lhasa, representing an ancient civilization, is, to me, a long reel of negatives of various pictures. Looking at them, I seem to see flashes of a fine day with an azure sky, a stormy day with scurrying clouds, intrigue and rivalry between aristocrats, and the glitter of sabers.... I seem to feel the strong atmosphere of sanctity of this holy city of Buddhism and gaze at the receding backs of throngs of pilgrims. I even seem to hear vendors hawking their wares in Barkor Street.... Old Lhasa was a Lhasa of monks, a Lhasa of nobles, a Lhasa of merchants, beggars, pilgrims and adventurers.

Originally the capital of the Tubo Kingdom, Lhasa dates back at least 1300 to 1400 years. The history of

A map of Lhasa drawn in the Qing Dynasty (1644-1911).

human settlement in the Lhasa area, according to archeological findings so far, is as long as 3,000 or 4,000 years, with the oldest evidence of habitation being the Neolithic Chugong Ruins on the northern bank of the Lhasa River. Towards the end of the Neolithic period, metal wares began to appear. In A.D. 633, Songtsan Gampo united all the tribes on the Qinghai-Tibet Plateau, and established the Tubo Kingdom as a slave society. The chiefs of the various tribes met and chose Rasa (present-day Lhasa) to be the capital. It seems to have been a well-wooded and well-watered place at that time. The land was fertile, and there was plenty of game to be hunted. The heyday of the Tubo Kingdom was during the reign of Trisong Detsen (742–797), the fifth king.

The original name of Lhasa was

A clay pot unearthed from the Chugong ruins.

This picture, preserved in the Norbu Lingka, shows metal workers in the olden days.*

A map of Lhasa made in the early 20th century. The basic layout of the city has remained unchanged since then.

Wotang. The word Rasa, which often appears in historical records, literally means "goat" and "earth." It probably refers to the legend that goats carried earth to build the Jokhang Monastery. The name Lhasa (literally "sacred land") came into being later, when Buddhism became the dominant religion in Tibet.

The establishment of Lhasa as the capital by Songtsan Gampo symbolized the end of strife between the different Tibetan tribes. People started to live a peaceful, settled life, and rules for society were drawn up. The social progress made during this period can be detected at various archeological sites: the cliff carvings at Chakpori (Medicine King) Hill, the Tralhalupuk Grottoes, the ruins of Pabongka, where the Tibetan script was created by Thonmi Sambhota, and others. Such data attest to the great material and social progress made in that period, and show that early Tibetan his-

The golden pinnacle of the Jokhang Monastery.* (1957)

tory paralleled what was happening in the Central Plains at roughly the same time. Previous to the establishment of the Tubo Kingdom, there had been a period of strife among the Tibetans similar to that of the Central Plains before Emperor Qin Shihuang (first emperor of the Qin Dynasty) unified China and ended the chaos of the Spring and Autumn (770-476 BC) and the War-

The old town of Lhasa, seen from the Potala Palace. * (1957)

Chakpori (Medicine King) Hill lies to the southwest of Lhasa. On top of this hill, there is a school of traditional Tibetan medicine. * (1957)

Stone carvings of the Buddha on Chakpori Hill, under renovation. * (1957)

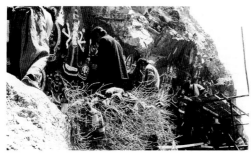

ring States (476-221 BC) periods. This was well summed up by an elderly official of the Tibet Archives whom I met during my trip there: "When the Interior Land is prosperous and powerful, Tibet is peaceful. When the Interior Land is in chaos, Tibet is in upheaval."

The Tubo Kingdom lasted for 300 to 400 years. When it collapsed, Tibet was ruled by contending chieftains from 969 to 1246. During the Song Dynasty (960-1279), which was a weak power, all that remained of connections between Tibet and the Central Plains seems to have been limited to trade in tea and horses. During the Sagya Period, in 13th century, when Tibet's political center moved westward, Tibet was officially incorporated into the territory of China's Yuan Dynasty. Some 130,000 clans in Tibet were given noble titles. Lhasa became one of the manorial estates bestowed on a man named Tshe-sbang, who was head of 10,000 households. The manorial system was abolished during the Ming Dynasty (1358-1644), but an administrative office was set up in Lhasa, and a policy of "giving more honorific noble titles and pooling more efforts for building the town" was adopted. The

Qing Dynasty (1644-1911) court fostered and supported the Gelug Sect of Tibetan Buddhism, which was centered and rose in Lhasa more than 600 years ago, and encouraged the formation of a theocratic socio-political structure. The grand monasteries of Drepung ('Brasspungs), Gandan (Dga'-ldan) and Sera were built in Lhasa in this period. With the backing of the Qing court,

Left: Statue of Thonmi Sambhota in the Cave of the Dharma King in the Potala Palace. It is said to have been made in the Tubo period. * (1957).

Lozang Gyatso (1617-1682), the fifth Dalai Lama, was the first autocrat under this new system, which lasted up until the mid-20th century.

The best photographs of old Lhasa were taken by Dainzin Gyatso, the 10th Living Buddha Demo, born in 1901. In addition to using this data, I made many visits to Lhasa, and did a lot of other preparations, including reading once again *The Demise of the Lamaist State*

Right: The Pabongka Monastery is located on Mount Nyangrain on the northern outskirts of Lhasa. It is said that Thonmi Sambhota created the Tibetan script in this monastery in the early Tubo period. * (1957)

by Melvyn C. Goldstein, a huge work consisting of more than 700,000 characters in the Chinese version. I limited my coverage of the subject to the first half of the 20th century. During the preparation work, sometimes I could not help laughing at myself, a resident of

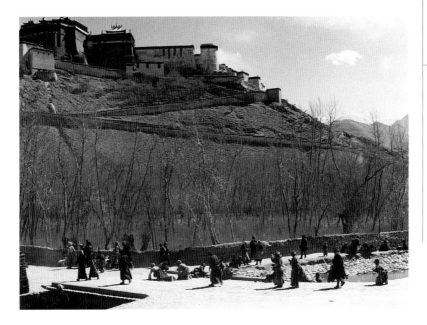

Pilgrims prostrate themselves to show their devotion as they make a circuit of the Potala Palace. * (1957)

Lhasa for more than 20 years, for my ignorance of the city. Perhaps I had too often turned my eyes far beyond the city to the countryside or pastureland, and Lhasa itself had become blurred.

The Potala Palace in snow. * (1956)

The Potala Palace at dawn. * (1957)

The 30th day of the second month by the Tibetan calendar is the anniversary of the death of the fifth Dalai Lama. On this day, a grand ceremony is held in Lhasa. The picture shows a huge *tangka* (scroll painting) on display on one such occasion, on the southern wall of the Potala Palace. * (1957)

An elephant parades the streets to commemorate the anniversary of the death of the fifth Dalai Lama. This elephant was kept in an elephant house by the Dragon King Pool behind the Potala Palace until the early 1960s. * (1957)

The Great Sutra Hall of the Drepung Monastery in Lhasa. * (1957)

A panorama of the Gandan Monastery, one of the three leading monasteries in Tibet. It is located 30 km to the east of Lhasa. This is the only Tibetan monastery which was destroyed during the "cultural revolution" (1966-1976). It was rebuilt in the 1980s. * (1959)

The 13ᵗʰ Dalai Lama with Charles Bell of Britain.

Why Was the Door of the Sacred City Closed?

First of all, I need to dwell for a while on the historical background, in order to elaborate on a feature of Lhasa which makes it so different from other cities in China. This feature enabled many Western explorers to write a large number of books, and more books have been written by later generations about those books themselves.

Only a little over 20 years ago, in the 1970s, Tibet was still regarded as a place of mystery. This was the result of poor communications and few exchanges between Tibet and the outside world. But since China adopted the policy of reform and opening to the outside world in the late 1970s, and particularly with the development of tourism, this situation has changed drastically. Tibet is no longer a "land of mystery." The reason Lhasa became so famous throughout the world

The Rongbu glacier on Mount Qomolangma (Mt. Everest), on the northern side of the Himalayas.
* (1960)

(primarily in the West) was, apart from the initial enthusiasm for a region unknown, that the door to Lhasa was closed. The more Tibet wanted to shut strangers out, the more they wanted to get in. The more the risks and failures, the more the stimulation and challenges. Such a mentality is ingrained in the composition of Westerners, ancient and modern. The tightly shut door itself was a focus of excitement. What was hidden behind the door? This further aroused their curiosity. The mystery was further spread and exaggerated. No matter from which direction they came, all the explorers who came by crossing the Himalayas in the south, the Qinghai-Tibet Plateau in the north, or rivers and mountains in the east were without exception stopped by the closed door of the sacred city. This made those

The Potala Palace, an architectural wonder of the world. (Photo by Zhang Ying)

explorers' curiosity all the more intense, and made Tibet and Lhasa even more intriguing.

Lhasa was quite willing to open to the outside world in the early days. Up until the 19th century, Lhasa welcomed foreigners, including Muslim and Christian missionaries. The first Muslim known to have reached Lhasa came from Kashmir, during the reign of the fifth Dalai Lama, some 400 years ago. He often prayed at the foot of Mount Ganpe in the northwestern suburbs of the city. The fifth Dalai Lama admired his devotion, and gave him a piece of land in the western suburbs so that he could have a better place to practice his religion, and he was exempted from all taxes and corvee labor. Such hospitality attracted more Muslims to Lhasa. Soon, a mosque and a cemetery were constructed, which attracted even more Muslims from Kashmir, Ladakh, Nepal and Sikkim to do business in Lhasa. Many Muslims, including some from the Central Plains, settled down there. They were disciplined, kept a low profile and had good relations with the local Tibetans. They never advocated their religion outside their own community. Most of them engaged in service work, and gradually they merged into the life of Lhasa. Politically, Islam had little influence in Tibet. However, its culture took root in Lhasa. Two mosques, one large and one small, stand side by side today in Barkor Street.

Several groups of Christian missionaries reached Lhasa during the Middle Ages. Some of them lived in Lhasa for scores of years. Like the Muslims, they were welcomed at first. The

Lieutenant Montgomery.

Czarist Russian officer Nilolay Prjevalsky, who invaded Tibet several times but failed to reach Lhasa.

seventh Dalai Lama and two regents before and after him, respectively, became very interested in Christianity. They were allowed to build churches and proselytize. Pholhanas, who was in charge of the political affairs of Tibet, ordered that Christian churches be protected and exempted the priests from certain taxes and corvee labor. But as the influence of Christianity spread, and the number of converts increased, a clash with the established Buddhist faith became inevitable. Finally, waves of persecution, involving the demolition of churches and the expulsion of foreign missionaries, exterminated Christianity in Tibet.

This left an indelible impression on the Tibetan people. Religious differences have long been more important to them than racial ones. After that, Tibetans, the monks in particular, mistrusted Westerners. Events in modern and contemporary history have proved that the Westerners truly had ulterior motives.

This episode also indicated that entry into Tibet was conditional. The very first condition was that the principle of the religious life of the Tibetan people must not be interfered with.

Tibet is said to have been turned into a forbidden zone after Qing troops had defeated a Nepalese invasion in the late 18th century. The victory strengthened the control of the Central Government in the hinterland over Tibet. Because of the rise of the

Francis Young-husband with his family, 1904. Young-husband led a British invasion force into Tibet in the same year.

Western powers, which threatened China's local interests, the Qing court decided to close Tibet to foreigners. This was in compliance with the basic closed-door policy of the late Qing Dynasty. This decision was naturally hailed by the Tibetan government. With natural barriers and the determination to block the infiltration of Westerners, Tibet seemed to feel secure in an absolutely isolated environment.

French woman explorer Alexandra David-Neel and her adopted son, a young Tibetan monk Aphur Yongden, in front of the Potala Palace. In the 1920s, she disguised herself as a Buddhist pilgrim, and entered Lhasa.

However, the door of Tibet was forced open by a British army officer named Francis Younghusband, who led an armed expedition into Tibet in 1904. A Western reporter exulted, "Today is probably the first time in world history that Lhasa has been mentioned as the place of release of a piece of news." It was a moment of indig-nation, disgrace, disappointment and despair for Lhasa, Tibet and China.

Before that, the Tibetan government and Buddhist monks had put up a heroic

Annie Tailor and her Tibetan servant Pontso. A dedicated British worker for the China Inland Mission, Tailor was denied entry to Lhasa.

British writer Peter Hopkirk, author of *Trespassers on the Roof of the World.*

fight against the invaders. However, there were people who hampered their efforts. One of them was the Qing Court's High Commissioner (Amban) You Tai, who disgracefully forced the Tibetan government to sign an agreement with the aggressors....

Later on, the door of Tibet was closed to the Han Chinese for a period of seven or eight years, during which time there were two mass expulsions of the latter from Tibet. Much of this period is covered in this book. This is called by some Westerners a period of "*de facto* independence of Tibet." But what actually happened was very complicated. In the historical circumstances of the time, no one in the Central Government knew who was who in Tibetan Gaxag government. Instigated by the imperialist powers headed by Britain, a few people tried hard to seek independent status. But, no matter whether from the point of view of historical relations, feelings between nationalities, geopolitics or international standards, how could Tibet be severed from China? The so-called internationalization of the "Tibet issue" originated in that period. Some people regarded the loss of the "kingdom of the monks" as a loss akin to that of the Garden of Eden. This, unfortunately, has inevitably given a strong political tinge to this book about Old Lhasa.

Enshrined in the Sasum Namgyel Mansion of the Potala Palace are a tablet wishing long life to the Qing Dynasty Emperor Qianlong and a portrait of him. Since the seventh Dalai Lama, Kelzang Gyatso, it has been a tradition that the Dalai Lamas would pay homage here on the third day of the first month by the Tibetan calendar. The ceremony of drawing lots from the golden urn to decide on the reincarnation of the Dalai Lama is also held here. * (1957)

The Potala Palace in the 1950s

The Living Buddha Demo Incident

In 1888, Tibetan troops and militia fought fiercely against British invaders, but were defeated at the battle of Mount Lungdo in 1888. As a result, first Sikkim and then Bhutan were lost to the imperialists. The Qing Dynasty was weak, and the fate of the country was at stake. Just at this juncture, in Lhasa a serious incident known as the "Demo Incident" took place. Whatever the truth of the matter, the young 13th Dalai Lama made this incident an excuse to start an internal crackdown. A century later, the people of Tibet are still divided about what happened, and there are some who say that the misfortunes that befell Tibet afterwards were retribution for the death of the ninth Demo.

During the 200 years from the sixth Dalai Lama to the 12th Dalai Lama, all the Dalai Lamas except for the seventh and eighth, who lived into their early forties, all died either in childhood or not long afterwards. It is likely that they were victims of power struggles involving regents.

For nine years until the 13th Dalai Lama was of age to assume the throne, the ninth Living Buddha Demo Hutuktu succeeded Living Buddha Gundeling as regent. During his years in power, the ninth Demo accumulated wealth exceeding even that of the Gaxag, the Tibetan.

When the Dalai Lama came of age and assumed the throne, Demo Hutuktu's political rivals saw their chance to topple him. They accused his nephew Norbu Tsering of a plot to murder the Dalai Lama. The crime Norbu Tsering was accused of was said to have been concocted in typical Tibetan fashion – by resorting to primitive witchcraft: The name and date of birth of the Dalai Lama had been written on a piece of paper over which an evil incantation had been pronounced. The piece of paper had then been sewn into the sole of one of a pair of boots presented as a gift to the Dalai Lama. As a result of this charge, all the property of the Demo Hutuktu, including monasteries and over 50 manorial estates, was confiscated. His title of Living Buddha Demo Hutuktu was abolished. He

The 13th Dalai Lama (early 20th century).

Ekai Kawaguchi, a Japanese monk, entered Tibet in disguise in the early 20th century. He later wrote a book about his adventures, titled *A Secret Trip to Tibet.*

himself, his nephew and others of his clan all died in prison. The wife of Norbu Tsering was pilloried in Barkor Street for seven days before being sent in exile. This latter incident was witnessed by a Japanese monk named Ekai Kawaguchi, who also reported seeing some 20 other people in shackles and hearing of the executions of 16 others and much more people exiled, all apparently involved in the plot.

However, the title of Living Buddha Demo was resurrected later. In fact, one of the 10th Living Buddha Demo's nephews worked with me as a photographer for more than 20 years, and he assured me that the whole incident was a scheme to wrest the wealth of the ninth Living Buddha Demo.

The 13th Dalai Lama bestowed the title on Dainzin Gyatso, one of his cousins. Dainzin Gyatso later became Tibet's first native photographer.

It was at the decree of Qing Dynasty Emperor Qianlong in 1746 that the seventh Living Buddha Demo began to exercise power on behalf of the Dalai Lama in the capacity of regent. From that time on, the Living Buddha Demo remained close to the Qing Court. But after the Qing Dynasty came to an end in 1911, the 13th Dalai Lama once more abolished the title of Living Buddha Demo, and Dainzin Gyatso lost everything overnight. Penniless, he continued his religious studies, and acquired the Lha-rams-pa (the highest degree among doctors of divinity) at the Drepung Monastery.

A turning point in his life came when he met a photographer from Nepal. This man had fallen severely ill, and had been carried to the rock on the northern outskirts of Lhasa on which corpses were dismembered and left for the vultures to eat. He miraculously revived, but, as Tibetan custom decreed that a person who came

back from the dead was not allowed to enter his home again, he became a vagabond. He was taken in by Dainzin Gyatso, to whom he taught the art of photography. This was in the 1920s, when a typical camera was as long as half a meter and very heavy. Its body was made of wooden planks, while the lens consisted of three thick pieces of glass. The lens and the body were connected by a leather tube. Attached to the body was a film compartment which could hold a 15cm x 15cm sensitive sheet. The sheet had to be changed for each shot. There were only two speeds: B and 1/15 of a second.

There was not much business for photographers in Tibet in those days, as the local people were very superstitious and thought that a photograph of a person captured his or her soul. It was not until the 1930s that Dainzin Gyatso had the opportunity to photograph the people of Tibet as well as the scenery and examples of everyday life. With a Carbine camera, the most advanced camera at that time, he visited towns and

Yutok Bridge, located in the west of Barkor Street, is one of Lhasa's ancient structures. It is locally known as the Glazed Tile Bridge, as its roof is covered with glazed tiles. It is now in the compound of the Lhasa Customs House. * (1957)

villages all over Tibet. The small copper-and-wood camera was very handy, and its speed reached 1/250 of a second.

Dainzin Gyatso took pictures of people of all social strata, and caught life from various angles and at different periods. Eventually, he had four cupboards full of negatives. Unfortunately, they were set on fire during the "cultural revolution" (1966-1976). Luckily, his son Bangphyug Dorje rescued more than 400 negatives from a pile of ashes and rubbish. Bangphyug Dorje himself became a photographer.

Yutok Yonten Gonpo, known as the founder of Tibetan medicine. * (1957)

Craftsmen of the Sholdoru metal workers' guild. (1920s)

The sutra library in the Potala Palace. * (1957)

Chapter 2
Past Ages

Aristocrats wear "pearl-decorated robes" at a New Year's banquet held in the Potala Palace.
This attire dates back to the age of Songtsan Gampo. *

Thepungang, a narrow alleyway in Lhasa. * (1957)

The Rise and Fall of the Tibetan Nobility

The nobility of old Tibet lived mostly in sumptuous mansions on Barkor Street. After many years of renovation, most of them are now well preserved, although a few have been demolished. Architecturally, they are by and large similar to one another in layout, resembling the *siheyuan* (courtyard houses) of the Han people, and have a framework consisting of "four beams and eight pillars." The main building, which always faces south, is three or four stories high. Around the yard are rooms connected by corridors leading to the yard. Due to a severe shortage of building materials, glass was not used for window panes, transparent paper or light cloth being used instead.

Nobles and their servants made up the main body of the local residents of Lhasa. A nobleman would also have grand manorial estates in the countryside. There,

Aristocratic ladies in formal dress (1920s or 1930s).

he had warehouses, granaries, stables, workshops, and even a prison for locking up unruly serfs. A manorial estate was virtually a self-reliant economy, and was governed by its own autonomous rules.

In 1920s and 1930s, and again in 1950s, there were two migrations by Tibetan nobles away from Barkor Street to the suburbs, where they built villas. They planted pine trees, fruit trees and willows in their large gardens. They imitated the British way of life, which they had learned from contacts with India. The beams they used for building their houses were light iron rails imported from India by trains of pack

Adopting a stiff pose for an early photograph.

Aristocratic ladies and their children in old Tibet. *

Triring Jigme, a senior official of the Gaxag Government of Tibet, uses a movie camera. This photo was taken by Chen Zonglie, a reporter of Xinhua News Agency, in the 1950s. *

animals. Besides, they started to bring in glass panes and window frames, also from India. Now their villas were bright and spacious. The second wave of migration to the suburbs was caused by the new government offering large sums of money to purchase mansions on Barkor Street to be used as office buildings.

When the 13th Dalai Lama came to power, he pressed forward with new policies, and for a time the nobles of Lhasa became very reform-minded. In the forefront of the reforms was a family headed by Triring. This family had migrated to Lhasa from Sikkim. In the past, Sikkim had been under the jurisdiction of Tibet, and people from Sikkim had often served in the Tibetan government and owned estates in Tibet. But while Triring was living in Lhasa, Sikkim was seized by the

Ladies and children of Charong's clan. The woman on the left, Rinchen Drolma, the daughter of Charong, later settled in India, and wrote a book titled, *Daughters of the Snowy Mountains.* *

British government of India, so he was unable to go back home. His eldest son Triring Jigme was a talented young man with a liberal mind. He took the lead in building villas on the outskirts of Lhasa, and designed the Norbu Lingka (the summer palace of the Dalai Lamas). He also designed golden-laced hats and more practical skirts for Tibetan women.

The coats of noblemen in old Tibet had long sleeves, indicating that they never did any manual labor. Farming was left to serfs. There was a man named Charong Dasang Zhamdui, who was a nobleman as well as an influential merchant. He had been born a serf, and never lost his love for growing things. Though a rich man, he liked to till his own land and grow vegetables. With glass and vegetable seeds from India, he built a greenhouse. He gave a cauliflower — a plant never seen in Tibet before in the 1930s — to his daughter's parents-in-law. The recipients of Charong Dasang's cauliflower asked him whether it was a flower

An aristocratic tea party. * (1956)

A Tibetan banquet in the 1930s. Well-off Tibetans in those days ate beef, mutton and cooked rice mixed with butter.

or a vegetable. The amused Charong Dasang sent someone over to show them how to cook the cauliflower.

What would usually be on the dining-table in a noble's home? Mutton and beef were traditional dishes. Apart from these, there were locally produced vegetables such as potato and *yuangen* (similar to a turnip). Other vegetables were collectively called "refined vegetables." Beverages included sweet tea, coffee and red wine. Common condiments were Chinese prickly ash and curry, which had been introduced from other countries.

The rights and interests of hereditary aristocrats were protected by Tibetan laws for centuries. As long as a noble did not commit any serious crime, he would be sure to make an easy and comfortable living off his manorial estates. He was entitled to education in a private school, and when he grew up he had right to serve in the government. He could assume the headship of a monastery, and would have a chance to be chosen as the reincarnation of a Living Buddha.

However, historical changes could be catastrophic

for the Tibet's ruling class. A large number of aristocrats of the Tubo Kingdom perished with the collapse of the regime. This was followed by a period of several hundred years, during which Tibet was carved up and ruled by various local powers. They were, either temporal or religious, recognized later by the imperial court of the Yuan Dynasty and impe-

The young Charong with his wife.

rial decrees gave them the right to own farmland and serfs. In modern times, the Tibetan aristocracy has all but disappeared.

The rise of a new nobility was particularly clear after the fifth Dalai Lama came to power. Especially the clan to which the new ruler belonged gained in wealth and prestige.

On the other hand, the extinction of a clan is exemplified by the history of the Ngapoi, which was once the most powerful family group in the Gongbo area. In the mid-18th century, the head of the clan and all his immediate family were put to death after

A couple pose for a photo.

the head of the clan had fallen foul of the Dalai Lama. His manorial estates were confiscated and given to someone else. The aristocratic name of Ngapoi continued, but there was no direct connection with the once-mighty Ngapoi of Gongbo.

Shekarling living in Tsang was ennobled because of his exploits in the war against the chief of Korga. A decree

In later life, Charong abandoned his official career to engage in trade, at which he was very successful. *

was issued that his posterity was entitled to inherit this title. So all of a sudden, Shekarling became a famous noble name. But a hundred years later, this clan declined, and disappeared. People would have forgotten this name if it were not for a man of this clan who went to Lhasa as a beggar and emerged a most talented man after assiduous studies there. His learning was appreciated by the 13th Dalai Lama, and the young man was accepted into the government, and enjoyed rapid promotion. He is still remembered because of a moving poem about him titled, *In Memory of Lhasa,* by Shekar Migyur Lhundrup.

The son-in-law system also went through a gradual course of evolution. In old Tibet, a son-in-law was regarded as equal to a son in family status. When discussing this topic, the two renowned clans Xazha and Charong are often cited as examples. In the early 18th

Karde, Charong's daughter, wife of Xazha.

The villa of Soikang, a renowned noble who later became Kalon. * (1957)

century, a man named Wangqug Gyaibo, who had been a monk, returned to secular life and married into the family of Xazha, thus becoming a son-in-law of the clan and inheriting a noble title. Later, he became a Kalon and then a regent. It so happened that he had no son, so he adopted his nephew Tsering Wangchuk as his son. On the strength of being a member of the Xazha clan, Tsering Wangchuk became a Kalon too. He was later dismissed and sent into exile, and his property was confiscated. It was many years before the clan began to restore its social status and recover some of its land. The only daughter of Tsering Wangchuk inherited the name Xazha, which was then passed on to her husband and again passed on to Benjor Doje, the son-in-law of the next generation.

Charong, a famous Kalon and concurrently the commander-in-chief of the Tibetan army in the early 20th century, was also a son-in-law of a noble family. His real name was Dasang Zhamdui, and he was from a poor family. When he grew up, he

served as a bodyguard of the 13th Dalai Lama. In 1912, suspecting treachery on the part of the leader of the Charong clan, the 13th Dalai Lama had the latter and his son executed, and bestowed on Dasang Zhamdui the name of Charong, as well as all the Charong manorial estates.

Girls from aristocratic families were chosen to be attendants at important banquets. *

It seems that what was important in Tibetan tradition was land and not blood lineage, the clan and not the individual. It is very difficult to trace back the history of a Tibetan clan because of absence of original family records. Details of people and events of even a few generations ago are quite vague. In some historical records, one often comes across the names of residences only. At most, there would be a radical "ba"

Sakya Dharma-raja
and his wife. *

(person) after the name of a residence. So it would be quite impossible to know who was who. In addition, generations are often miscalculated. Luckily, we are quite clear about the persons and events in this book, since the period under scrutiny is relatively recent.

Apart from the title to land and people, Tibetan

An aristocratic lady
and her servant. *

nobles were also entitled to become officials. These positions were unsalaried, but whether in the central government in Lhasa or as a county magistrate, the opportunities for amassing wealth through graft were enormous. People of humble birth were ineligible for official jobs, unless they were ennobled first, like Charong Dasang Zhamdui. In modern times, there is an instance of a wealthy merchant, a certain Sangdutsang, who was a commoner and who purchased an official position before being given an aristocratic title. Up until one or two centuries ago, official positions were hereditary too; a son automatically succeeded to his father's official position. Later reforms ensured, at least in principle, that a member of the nobility started from a low-ranking post and rose gradually. When he reached a certain rung on the ladder, his personal ability and the influence of his clan became important criteria for further promotion.

Costume for nobles, showing the influence of Qing Dynasty official attire.

However, the higher one climbed, the more risks one faced, as the power struggle intensified.

In 1959, when Tibet shook off its long history of feudal serfdom, there were, according to a census, about 200 noble clans. Together with the senior monks and the personnel of the Gaxag government, they owned almost all the farmland in Tibet.

The 200 noble clans had originated in the area between Lhasa and Xigaze. They had their manorial estates in the nearby countryside, and pasturelands in northern Tibet. But no matter where their properties were located, almost all of them preferred to live in Lhasa, leaving the management of their estates to stewards.

Ganden Tripa on an inspection tour. *1957

A nobleman rides on a white horse, attended by servants on foot holding prayer flags.

Much has been said about the miserable life of serfs. It is basically true. But, since they are not part of old Lhasa, I will not go into details. However, it is worth reminding the reader that a commoner's fate was controlled by someone else, and his life was, as a result, unbelievably miserable and poverty-stricken. A serf might be a debtor when he was born, for one of his forefathers might have borrowed some barley many years before, which had snowballed into a huge debt under the usurious system practiced at that time. That was why the reform of 1959 was hailed by poor Tibetans.

A procession of a nobleman and his servants.

A serf pays the poll tax for his new-born baby. * (1958)

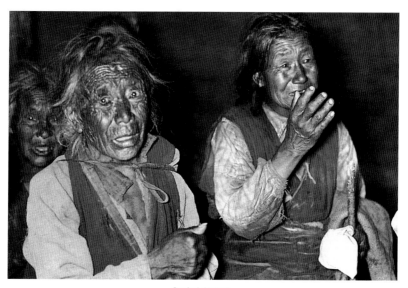

Serfs * (1958)

The Monlam Prayer Festival (Monlam Chenmo) is held in Lhasa in the first month by the traditional Tibetan calendar. Monks come from all parts of the country to attend the ceremony. * (1957)

Monlam Prayer
Festival * (1958)

A World of Lamas

After the "cultural revolution" came to an end in 1976, we drove along the Qinghai–Tibet Road all the way to Lhasa. When the magnificent Potala Palace, Drepung Monastery, Sera Monastery, Norbu Lingka and Jokhang Monastery came into view, we felt much relieved. But there was a sharp contrast between those palaces and monasteries, and the shabby residences along the way, as well as in Lhasa. When I stepped into those resplendent halls and saw pagodas made of pure gold, I could not help thinking that all the wealth of Tibet was probably stored there.

The reason Lhasa became known as a sacred city was that it was home to so many monasteries and so many monks. Besides, it was where the Dalai Lama, supposedly a reincarnation of the Goddess of Mercy (Avalokitesvara), resided. Guanyin was supposed to

Gilded funerary stupa containing the body of the 5th Dalai Lama. The gold used for it weighs 5. 5 kg. The precious stones inlaid in this stupa are more valuable than the gold. * 1957

oversee the present and future of mankind. In 1951, when Lhasa was liberated peacefully, there were about 20,000 monks in the three major monasteries of Gandan, Sera and Drepung, and the four great *ling* (palaces) of Gundeling, Dangyailing, Cemoinling and Cejoiling. So there were more monks than lay people in Lhasa at that time. The monasteries, just like the aristocratic clans, also owned manorial estates and serfs. In fact, the total amount of farmland they owned was larger than that owned by the nobles, accounting for 37% of Tibet's arable land. The Drepung Monastery alone, which was the largest, had more than 10,000 monks, 185 manorial estates, 20,000 serfs, 300 pastures and 16,000 herdsmen. It had subsidiary mon-asteries scattered all over Tibet. Apart from the annual revenue from its manorial estates, it also earned money by engaging in trade and commerce, and money lending. Therefore, a monastery was equal to a semi-autono-

The funerary stupa for the 13th Dalai Lama, made in 1934, is 14 m high. The stupa is coated with 590 kg of gold. The value of the precious stones inlaid in this stupa is ten times that of the gold. It is the most elaborate of the eight funerary stupas in the Potala Palace. * 1957

mous or virtually autonomous organization as far as its social status was concerned. It was essentially an economic conglomerate.

Monks of the three major monasteries and belonging to all the various sects of Tibetan Buddhism played an important role not only in religious activities but also in political affairs. At times, their political role could be decisive. The Gelug Sect, headed by the Dalai Lama, was the dominant sect in Tibetan Buddhism.

People have different opinions on Tibetan Buddhism. Some are fascinated by it, while others take a completely negative attitude. There are also people whose minds are divided. But most people find it mysterious, which arouses their curiosity. Compared with Buddhism in other parts of the world, Tibetan Buddhism is indeed unique in various ways: its system of reincarnation of Living Buddhas, the practice of the unfathomable Esoteric Buddhism, its process of becoming Buddha Guardians, its rituals, its knowledge which covers almost everything under the sun, and the form of examination and debate.... The senior monks, for instance, are in fact learned people. They have attained a degree of profound learning after years of hard study and debating. The debates over scriptures are particularly interesting. One monk fires a question and another will answer it or challenge the questioner with another question. With each question

A scripture debate. *

A scripture debate is held in front of the Jokhang Monastery. An iron pole monk (Tshogchen Shango), acting as a security guard, can be seen in the picture. * (1957)

or each answer, a clap of the hands is made by the speaker to emphasize his point. The rhythm of such debates is rapid, and the atmosphere tense. If a monk falters in answering or what he says does not hold water, he is lost.

The "iron pole monks" (locally known as "Tshogchen Shango") in Tibetan monasteries was quite a sight. Such monks were usually very tall and robust, and wore voluminous robes. They deliberately wore a stern expression, particularly in public, as though they were acting. The name iron pole monk itself indicates that they were posted to maintain order. During the annual Monlam Prayer Festival, which lasts for 21 days in the first month of the Tibetan calendar, the "mayor" of Lhasa would surrender his power to the Iron pole monks of the

Iron pole monks of the Drepung Monastery. * (1957)

Iron pole monks of the Drepung Monastery. * (1957)

Iron pole monks clearing the way for a religious procession. * (1957)

Drepung Monastery to maintain order. They were supposed to be in charge of not only human beings but also deities. Wielding poles or whips, they stalked the streets and yelled at the top of their lungs. It was recorded that a Russian was whipped by them in 1901 and a Frenchman hit by their poles in 1924 in the streets of Lhasa.

In the old days, the monasteries kept teams of "Martial Monks". It was estimated that there were about 2,000 such monks in the three major monasteries. Their main task was not learning but practice of martial arts. They functioned as manual laborers in monasteries and had to attend to all the hard and dirty work. Since they did not study the Buddhist scriptures, they would, of course, have no hope of becoming Living Buddhas. So their ambition was to become Buddha Guardians. I know a man with the title of Buddha Guardian, who lives in the Sangphu Monastery on the

An iron pole monk guards a Monlam Prayer Festival at the Jokhang Monastery. * (1957)

On the occasion of the Monlam Prayer Festival, monks perform a ceremony in Barkor Street. * (1957)

southern bank of the Lhasa River. He used to be a monk in the Drepung Monastery. He was given the title because once he had shown signs of being possessed by a spirit. I heard that a Martial Monk was given the title because he had kept murmuring about becoming a Buddha Guardian, and he once made a terrible face and jumped into the Lhasa River when it was in full spate.

Trainee monks take a break for a meal at the Drepung Monastery. * (1958)

The ordinary people were terrified of the Martial Monks. As long as they protected the interests of their monasteries, they seemed to be allowed to do anything. They kept watch on the outside world as if there was imminent danger. They even dared to confront the Gaxag government or its army, and clashes happened from time to time. Because of the existence of these monks, monasteries in Lhasa seemed to give people the impression that all monks were militant and aggressive. There were two famous examples in modern history. On both occasions, monks of the Drepung and Sera monasteries, respectively, fought against troops of the Gaxag government. So, in a way, monas-

The monks are creating a sand mandala. *

teries were also organizations of a military nature.

In the 1920s, monks of the Drepung Monastery launched a demonstration against the Divine King (a title of the Dalai Lama). They got the upper hand at first. Several thousand monks rushed down the mountain where the Drepung Monastery stood, and marched and then charged into the Norbu Lingka. The 13th Dalai Lama immediately ordered his Commander-in-Chief Charong to drive them back to their monastery, which he did, without casualties. But an armed clash between monks of the Sera Monastery and the government army in the 1940s led to volleys of rifle and cannon shots, resulting in a great loss of life.

In 1947, when the patriotic Living Buddha Reting was arrested by the pro-British government, accused of being "pro-Han," the monks of the Sera monastery, his power base, threatened to attack the prison and rescue Reting. At the urging of Hugh Richardson, Britain's commercial representative in Gyangze, the Gaxag government, headed by Living Buddha Taktra,

Tibetan soldiers drill in the Potala Palace's Deyangshar Square. * (1957)

mobilized armed force to capture the monastery and put it under lock and key.

The religious groups represented by the three major monasteries were the direct beneficiaries of the theocratic socio-political structure, but sharp contradictions with such a society were inevitable. They constantly opposed the reforms attempted by the 13th Dalai Lama, Regent Reting and the Gaxag government. They were highly vigilant, and ready at any time to resist any moves which they thought might harm their interests. When it came to armed conflict, the monks were defeated every time, but they nevertheless managed to halt all attempts to alter the status quo.

In old Tibet, it was the dream of every child in the poverty-stricken villages to enter a monastery. That way, they would acquire learning, their social status would be enhanced, and they would say farewell to manual labor for good. The unique political system in

Tibet made the monasteries the guardians of the social order, and the monks as a group had tremendous political power. A good example of their power was the abolition of an English school in Lhasa as a result of the opposition of the three major monasteries. In 1943, the Gaxag government set up an English school in Lhasa at the request of Richardson, and entrusted the Briton to employ two English teachers. This was supported by the nobles (most of the school's 43 students were from aristocratic families), but it made the monks uneasy, as they believed that English language teaching was a threat to the existing social order. As a result of the monks' threats, the school was eventually closed after it had been in operation only five months. There are conflicting views on this incident: Some people point to it as an example of the reactionary conservatism of the monks, while others are mindful of the role played by the monasteries in battling against the British invaders early in the 20th century, and claim that the monks were more aware of the danger of British imperialism than the nobles of Tibet at that time.

During a Monlam Prayer Festival that lasted for 21 days, the three leading monasteries announced that power over the city of Lhasa belonged to them. The photo shows a Khan-po (abbot) making the public announcement to this effect. * (1957)

After Lungshar, a lay head of the Gaxag government, fell in 1934,

Guards of honor
blow horns. * (1958)

both regents from then to 1951 were Living Buddhas.
In a society where law is inadequate, power without
supervision inevitably leads to corruption. This is also
true of senior clergymen of any faith. The corruption
of the last regent Taktra Rimpoche is a typical example
of this.

When Taktra became regent he was almost 70.
Before that, he had been little known in political circles.
He had been noted for his indifference to fame and
gain, and his administrative office was probably the
poorest among such organizations in Lhasa. It was
pure coincidence that he took on a political role. What
happened was that the pro-British faction in the gov-

ernment ousted Living Buddha Reting, who was thought to be too loyal to China's Central Government, as regent, and the neutral and respected Taktra took his place, supposedly on a temporary basis. During the initial period of his term of office, Taktra seemed to be honest in handling administrative affairs. But before long, power began to corrupt him. He and his cronies accepted bribes, sold official titles and amassed wealth in all sorts of other crooked ways. His degradation reached such a point that he imprisoned and poisoned Reting, and spearheaded the forces working for independence for Tibet in the late 1940s. However, his schemes went awry, and he died in disgrace.

Tibetan monasteries pay great attention to the performance of religious music. The telescope trumpet and the sacred horn are the major musical instruments. The picture shows monks of the Sera Monastery playing musical instruments at a Monlam Prayer Festival. * (1957)

The two figures in the front of the picture are iron pole monks of the Drepung Monastery, which is responsible for keeping order during the Monlam Prayer Festival in Lhasa. (Photo by Zhang Ying, provided by Chen Zonglie)

Monks performing their daily sutra reading. The scriptures are written on pattra leaves.

Young monks at a religious ritual. * (1957)

At the Monlam Prayer Festival, monks chant sutras six times a day, wishing a happy and peaceful life for the people and prosperity for Buddhism. The photo shows monks chanting a sutra, led by Wenzed, in the square on the southern side of the Jokhang Monastery. * (1957)

A panoramic view of the Drepung Monastery * (1957)

Galdan Phobrang (Palace of Prosperity) of the Sera Monastery used to be where the 2nd to 5th Dalai Lamas lived. Later, it became the symbol of the local government. Finally, it was turned into the Gaxag. * (1957)

Kalon Trimoin was the most powerful man among the four Kalons in the 1930s.

The Gaxag Government

The local government of Tibet, known as Gaxag, represented the will and interests of the two large groups in Tibet, monks and noble laymen. At the same time, it was one of the major estate-holders itself. Together, the three of them owned all the land of Tibet. The Gaxag government was supposed to be the highest administrative body. Its power, however, was limited to administration of secular affairs; religious affairs were administered by monk officials. Sovereignty over both religious and temporal affairs was in the hands of the Divine King, i.e. the Dalai Lama, or his representative the regent. From the Gaxag government down to the county governments, monk and lay officials shared the administrative posts, with the former higher than the latter in rank. Under the Gaxag government and the religious organs, there were various bodies in charge

A scene of Barkor Street. The earring was the badge of an official. * (1957)

The Shol Lekhung at the foot of the Potala Palace. It was in charge of local administrative affairs and criminal cases. This organization was jointly headed by a monk official and a lay official appointed by the local government. * (1957)

The four Kalons in 1957: (from left to right) Ngapoi Nagwang Jigme, Xaisur Gyumey Dorje, Neuxar Thubten Thapa and Sampo Cewang Rinzin. *

Warriors in ancient uniform of the thousand-strong Tibetan army, which was divided into the Left Corps and the Right Corps with Soikang as its marshal in the 1940s. * (1957)

of the administration of finance and taxation. The office of the Gaxag was usually on the second floor of the Jokhang Monastery, but some of its functions were carried out in the Potala Palace or in offices called Shol at the foot of the Potala Palace, and in the Norbu Lingka. The monk and lay officials wore different robes. There were rules, going into minute detail, stipulating the different colors and materials of robes for the different ranks of officials, as well as the different kinds of precious stones which they were allowed to wear in their hair. However, all officials wore an earring in their left ear, which hung down over the shoulder. The earring differentiated them from commoners. Interestingly, each official carried a small cloth bag at his waist, containing a pair of chopsticks and a bowl. The date for changing into summer robes was the eighth day of the third month by the Tibetan calendar, while the date for changing into winter robes was the 25th day of the 10th month. This regulation was strictly followed.

Officials of the local government of Tibet: (from left to right) lay official Xaisur Gyumey Dorje, and monk officials Lobsang Zhaxi and Neuxar Thubten Thapa. * (1956)

In the city of Lhasa, there were parks known as *lingka* where lay and clerical officials gathered for parties. The *Lingka* Festival (World Incense Day) was held annually, hosted and funded by officials in turn. In summer, the officials would make appointments to go to a *lingka* with their whole families, all in their best clothes, especially the women. Tents were erected in clearings in the woods, segregated according to rank and sex. There was a great deal of ostentation in the ornaments and decorations for the tents, and it was not uncommon for a host to spend his life savings on one such party. Fortunately, since there were so many officials, the duty to host such a party would normally only come round once in a lifetime.

The party hosted by the Gagax government at the annual *Lingka* Festival was, of course, the most sumptuous. Professional dancers and singers were hired, at enormous expense. The feast was hosted in turn by the four Kalons. Each would try to outdo his predecessor of previous year. There were so many temporal and religious festivals, that it was said that officials spent half the year celebrating festivals. After the *Lingka* Festival, there came the

Golden Phobrang of the Norbu Lingka.* (1956)

Officers of the Tibetan army, monk officials and lay officials, in a photograph taken some time between 1920 and 1923. Sixth from the left is Charong. *

seven-day Shoton (Yogurt) Festival. Officials spent most of the summer at leisure out in the open. Old Lhasa was indeed a paradise for those who had power or money, but today the ordinary people of Tibet can enjoy such parties too, as they are entitled to a one-week Shoton Festival holiday, apart from statutory public holidays. Another long holiday is the Tibetan New Year, which again lasts for seven days.

The Gaxag is regarded as a local government because its nature and function were similar to that of a government. But it would be very difficult to consider it a government by either Chinese or Western standards as far as the structure of the organization or roles of officials are concerned. Except for those of the Dalai Lama, who was also known as the Divine King, and the regent, who was regarded as the governor of Tibet for a limited period of time, the duties and responsibilities of the officials are not clear. For instance, Lonchen and Srid-blon are translated "prime minister" by some Western Tibetologists. Both were new positions created by the 13th Dalai Lama for the purpose of striking a bal-

The four Kalons of the late 1940s: (from left) Namseling, Lukangwa, Ngapoi Nagwang Jigme and Shakabpa. *

ance of power. In practice, they had no real power. Likewise, it would be quite impossible to put the organizations of the Gaxag in the perspective of a government of today because of differences of political systems, structures and duties. Its function was a combination of religion and politics.

What is particularly strange about the Gaxag was that it was sometimes not in a ruling position when it came to political affairs, not to mention religious affairs. Administration of monasteries was not within its jurisdiction. Very often, it was only one part of a triangular power relationship formed together with the organized monasteries and the army. Sometimes, it allied with monasteries to contain and oppose the army; sometimes, it collaborated with the army in a struggle against the monasteries. When a Dalai Lama or a regent managed to exercise autocratic rule, the role of the Gaxag was even more limited. Then its functions were confined to handling documents.

Besides, because all the land and the people who worked on it belonged to their masters, the government's administrative work was extremely simple. Its primary

Rare Buddhist sutras written on pattra leaves. They were introduced into Tibet around the 10th century. Since it is damp and hot in India, no pattra leaf sutra has survived there. But the dry climate of Tibet has preserved many of them. * (1957)

work involved collection of taxes, and arrangement of corvee labor and religious activities, and related expenses.

One peculiar task of the Tibetan government was the investigation and collection of all sorts of information about strange happenings and mysterious signs. There are a large number of such reports and instructions stored in the Tibet Archives. For example, it had to be reported if a sheep gave birth to a litter of lambs, or a mule became pregnant. A sheep giving birth to two lambs or more was regarded as an auspicious sign, and the owner would be given a reward. A mule giving birth was regarded as a bad omen, and monks had to be invited to chant Buddhist scriptures to drive away the bad luck. In 1859, the Fiery Dragon Year by the Tibetan calendar, a couple in Xegar County gave birth to a son whose face was black on the right side and fair on the left. In addition, the baby had hair all over his body. A report about this baby was submitted to the Gaxag. Regent

Buddhist ritual bowls inlaid with silver filigree, made of human skulls.

Buddhist ritual objects made of human hand or arm bones. * (1957)

Reting thought it a bad omen, and instructed that a Buddhist ceremony be held to ward off any calamity. Another case was a report made by Sox County to the Gaxag that a newly born baby had white hair and white eyebrows. The Gaxag held that it was a bad omen, and instructed that the Kangyur Scripture must be chanted at a Buddhist ceremony to dispel the evil influence.

Officers and men of the Tibetan army and young aristocrats were quick to pick up new things in the early years of the 20th century. They learned

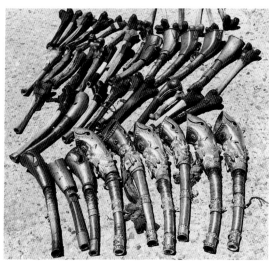

Sacred trumpets in Drepung Monastery made of virgins' leg bones collected by celestial burial masters. * (1957)

how to play football from British visitors, and playing football became somewhat fashionable — until the Gaxag issued a decree banning the sport. The reason? Some monk had noticed that the ball resembled the head of Sakyamuni, and deemed the kicking of such a divine image sacrilegious.

Another strange custom was that only the sun, the moon and the constellations were allowed to look down upon the supreme ruler, the Dalai Lama. One year, a British official in Lhasa fell ill, and the British government of India wanted to evacuate him to a hospital by helicopter. But the Tibetan government would not hear of it: No person was permitted to fly over the

head of the Dalai Lama. As a result, the Briton died of illness. A similar incident occurred during World War II, when a U.S. Air Force plane lost its way when flying over the Himalayas. The pilot and co-pilot parachuted to safety, and were escorted to Lhasa by representatives of the government of the Republic of China. But on the way they narrowly escaped lynching at the hands of mobs of Tibetans, incensed that they had dared to look down on the Divine King from the sky.

Tibetans dressed as ancient warriors on the occasion of a Monlam Prayer Festival.

Whenever an important decision, political or religious, was to be made, oracles would be consulted. A sorcerer's mumbling words or some arcane gesture would be regarded as infallible....

Tibetans dressed as ancient warriors. * (1957)

On the 24th day of the first month by the Tibetan calendar, the last day of the Monlam Prayer Festival, Nechung Chosgyong, a leading sorcerer, goes to the Lubu Square to the west of the Jokhang Monastery to preside over a ceremony to expel evil spirits. * (1957)

Chapter 3
The Kaleidoscope of Barkor Street

Thepungang, an alleyway on Barkor Street.*

The Tang-Tubo Alliance Monument erected in AD 823, a token of the pledge of eternal peace between the Tibetan and Han peoples. * (1956)

Circular Road

Barkor in the Tibetan language means a circular route. So Barkor Street, as indicated by its name, is a circular road. Buddhist devotees also call it *Bodhi* Road. The flagstone-paved street is about one kilometer long, and is flanked by neatly arranged houses in typical Tibetan architectural style. Today, it is only a part of the old town of the city. But in the past, as shown on old maps of Lhasa, Barkor Street and its surrounding area comprised almost all of the city. The eastern, northern and western suburbs, where rows of buildings stand today, used to be stretches of grassland, marshes, woods and fields. So in the minds of Tibetan people, Lhasa became identified with Barkor Street.

Old Lhasa was the epitome of old Tibet. Every aspect of Tibet could be found there. Barkor Street was a community with the highest density of population and buildings in the whole of Tibet. The oldest and most magnificent building in Barkor Street is Jokhang Monastery, where a life-sized statue of Sakyamuni at the age of 12 is enshrined. It was brought by Princess Wencheng of the Tang Dynasty, 1,300 years ago, and first installed in the Ramoche Monastery.

In front of the Jokhang Monastery are located a stone stele and a willow tree, which are known as the Tang Stele and the Tang Willow Tree. The stele was erected about a thousand years ago to mark the end of a war and the formation of an alliance between the Tibetans and Han Chinese. The thousand-year-old willow tree died during the "cultural revolution." The dead branches are hung with Buddhist streamers and prayer scarves, as in the minds of the local residents its soul still exists.

The Tang Willow in front of the Jokhang Monastery is said to have been planted by Princess Wencheng in person. So it is also known as the Princess Willow. It was still living in the 1960s. Beside it stands the Tang-Tubo Alliance Monument. * (1956)

The Jokhang Monastery was first built in the seventh century. It remains virtually intact, despite over a thousand years of storm and stress in the history of Buddhism. We know through carbon-dating that most of the beams and rafters are the original ones; the others were replaced in the 1970s, when the monastery was renovated.

In the past, Barkor Street used to have seven large alleyways fanning out in all directions. With small lanes

The structure of the universe according to a Time Wheel Calendar. *

An ancient mural in the Jokhang Monastery showing sheep carrying earth to fill a lake to build the Jokhang Monastery. *

joining the alleyways, it resembled to a spider's web.

This street is always crowded with people who follow the main flow, always going in the same direction. The tall Tibetan-style buildings flanking the street are like the banks of a river, solid and majestic. There are also clusters of tents which

East Barkor Street. *

Scene of Barkor Street.

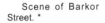

Scene of Barkor Street. *

serve as semi-permanent residences for those who have come here from afar. The tents in front of the Jokhang Monastery are home to people from Qinghai Province; the tents near the Ramoche Monastery on the northern part of the street are known as the Beggars' Tents, which also house many herdsmen from northern Tibet. Having passed the Upper and Lower Tantric Houses, and the Melu Monastery, one comes across the Black Yak Tents, for people from Khams-pa. In the eyes of the Lhasa residents, the people of northern Tibet are honest and well behaved, whereas the people of Khams-pa are aggressive. The northern side of Barkor East is where shops run by Nepalese are concentrated, and the southern side is full of shops and pharmacies run by Han Chinese. The latter shops are run mostly by people from Yunnan and Beijing. To the southeast of Barkor Street is the Muslim area. Barkor East is located right behind the Jokhang Monastery. There stands a yellow-colored building, which is locally known as the Yellow House. It was said to be the place of rendezvous for Tsangyang Gyatso, the sixth Dalai Lama, and his lover. Today, this building is used as a café, with the name *The Maiden*

Monks in front of the Jokhang Monastery at a Monlam Prayer Festival. *

written in Tibetan, Mandarin and English on its signboard. The name originates in a poem written by Tsangyang Gyatso. It goes like this:

> *Over that mountaintop in the east,*
> *Rises a serene moon,*
> *The face of the maiden,*
> *Appears in my heart.*

Different religions and ethnic cultures co-exist in peace in Lhasa. Not far from Barkor East, there stand two mosques, one small and one large. Around them is the settlement of Muslims from Gansu, Qinghai and Western Asia. It has been several hundred years since they settled in Tibet. Muslims have traditionally engaged in business here, including running teahouses, restaurants and groceries, and engaging in animal slaughtering.

A little further on, on Barkor South, there stands a building known as the Ngantsesha. This is the seat of the municipal government. The head of the Ngantsesha is known as the Miboin, which is translated as "mayor."

The principal duties and responsibilities of this organization in the old days were to maintain law and order and public sanitation, and inspect weights and measures in the market. The repair work on the embankments of the Lhasa River also came under its jurisdiction. However, important decisions were always submitted to the Gaxag government. The Miboin was more like the chief of police than the mayor of the city. When evidence was not sufficient in a case and it was difficult to make a ruling, the Miboin would toss a black and a white wooden dice – one for the plaintiff and one for the defendant. Whoever got the highest number would win the case. The loser would have to present a ceremonial scarf to the winner and apologize to him.

Barkor Street actually refers to a fairly large area. Apart from the trunk road, it also includes numerous alleyways. In the old days, various businesses were carried on in the alleyways such as sales of horses, weapons, local produce, etc. There were also 48 wine shops and seven kerosene stores. In addition, there were opium dens and places offering the services of prostitutes. It was generally the rich who could afford to smoke opium in those days, but finally the vice, along with gambling, was outlawed by both the high commissioners from the hinter-

Monks in Barkor Street during a Monlam Prayer Festival. *

The Tibetan opera *Princess Wencheng* is performed in the square of the Jokhang Monastery. * (1957)

land and the Dalai Lama. The relevant decrees are now housed in the local archives.

If you follow Barkor South, you will return to the starting point — the Jokhang Monastery. About a hundred meters to the west of the monastery is Tengyeling. Next to Tengyeling is Tibet's first post office, Drakhang. Lhasa started its postal service in modern times. Communication with the hinterland was speeded up by a land-sea route which went via India and Hong Kong, and vice versa. However, the mail had to be transported by pack horses and mules for about 500 km to reach the railhead in India. Still, it was faster than before.

There has been a postal system in Tibet, in fact,

since the Yuan Dynasty, which was improved during the Ming and Qing dynasties. The Central Government divided the daily speed for delivery of mails into four classes, according to the importance of the mail. The delivery speed for first-class mail was 300 km per day. Wind or snow, day or night, such items had to be delivered within the time limit. They were usually the most urgent documents of the Central Government. The speed for second-class mail was set at 250 km per day; for third-class mail, 200 km; and 150 km for fourth-class mail. Everybody knew that a dispatch rider was coming by the jangling of the bells attached to his waist. At night, as he approached a relay station, he would hold high a flaming torch to warn the next rider to get ready to take over.

A little further to the west of Drakhang stood a building, which used to be the office of the high commissioners. It was in the reign of Emperor Kangxi (1662-1722) of the Qing Dynasty that the system of dispatching high commissions by the Qing Court was established. For a period of 200 years, more than 100 high commissioners were appointed. Their performance had much to do with the power of the Qing Court. During the two anti-British invasions, high commissioners Sheng Tai and You Tai, who were brothers, played a capitulationist role, which was in compliance

Khyenrab Norbu, head of Mentsi Khang (Tibetan hospital), was a famous doctor of Tibetan medicine in the mid-20th century. After he became blind, he transmitted his medical theory orally. * (1956)

with the capitulationist line of the Qing Court: In 1888, during the first British armed attack on Tibet, Sheng Tai refused to back the resistance of the Tibetans, and lost Sikkim, which became a dependency of the British Empire. Sheng Tai died soon afterwards — of shame, it

The post office of old Tibet issued eight types of stamps. The illustration is a stamp with a value of two taels (one tael equals 31.25 g) of Tibetan silver. It is 7.6 cm by 6.3 cm, the biggest of the Tibetan stamps.

is said — and was succeeded by You Tai. In 1904, when British troops led by Col. Younghusband invaded Tibet, he stubbornly opposed the resistance war of the Tibetan people, led by the 13th Dalai Lama. When the invaders entered Lhasa, he became a lackey of the aggressors.

This man's diary is an important source of information about everyday life in Tibet at that time. In it, he recorded the weather and road conditions, and what he saw on his way to Tibet. During his stay in Lhasa, he kept a daily record of the weather, his changes of clothes, what precious stones he bought in the street and their

A letter delivered by sea via India with a Tibetan stamp bearing a dragon pattern and an Indian stamp franked in 1911.

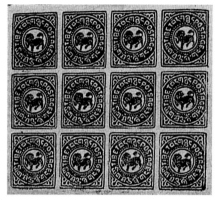

Ordinary stamps issued by the Dragkhang (post office). One sheet contained 12 stamps. The face value of each stamp was 7.5 cents. It is fiery purple in color.
*

prices, invitations to singsong girls and their names, and so forth.

The Jokhang Monastery is the destination of all pilgrims who come from far away. Around this monastery there are three circumambulation routes for devotees to pace while chanting Buddhist scriptures. Barkor Street serves as the intermediate circumambulation circle. The inner circumambulation circle refers to the corridors of the Jokhang Monastery, with the golden statue of Sakyamuni as its center. The outer circle, called Lingkor, leads clockwise around the city's pre-1950 limits, en-

The old Dragkhang (post office). * (1956)

compassing the mosques in the east, Linguo Road in the south, the Chakpori in the west and the Ramoche Monastery in the north. Worshippers come here from all parts of Tibet, Gansu, Yunnan, Sichuan and Qinghai. Every day, there are flows of worshippers going clockwise, some prostrating themselves from time to time on the ground. Occasionally, you may see a man holding up a finger that is on fire. This is another ancient practice, expressing devotion to Buddha.

Business in this street in ancient times must have been similar to what it is today. The street is now chock-a-block with shops and stalls with all sorts of things hanging or spread out in front. It is full of pedestrians, vendors, bargainers and window-shoppers.

The night curfew, announced by the firing of a cannon shot, left Barkor Street deserted. People would stay at home, playing cards or mahjong. The latter game

Pious devotees prostrate themselves in front of the Jokhang Monastery. This practice has been in existence for more than one thousand years. * (1957)

 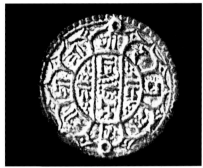

From the late 16th century to late 18th century, silver coins used in Tibet were made of Tibetan silver but minted in Nepal. A silver coin could also be cut into pieces and used. The coin on the left was minted in Nepal.

Counterfeit Tibetan coins once sparked a war between Tibet and Nepal. When the war ended, in 1792, the Qing Court authorized Tibet to build its own mint. The silver coin at top right was made in this mint.

had been introduced into Tibet by merchants from Yunnan, and was first taken up by aristocratic families. The traditional oil lamps were replaced for the most part, especially among the wealthy, by gas lamps in the late 19th century, but it was not until a hydro-electric power station was built on the northern outskirts of Lhasa in the 1930s that electricity entered the homes of the elite. On the occasions of the Butter Lamp Festival on 25th day of the 10th month by the Tibetan calendar and on the anniversary of death of Great Master Tsongkhapa, each and every house in Barkor Street lit a row of butter lamps placed on the roof. It was quite a sight to see the street brightly illuminated like this.

Except for outdoor activities on the occasions of major festivals, local residents of Lhasa were not allowed to go out at night, for security reasons. There were thieves too in the holy city. There was an islet in the Lhasa River, which was known as the Robber Woods. It was said to be a den of thieves. Anyone found loitering in the street after the curfew shot had been fired would be arrested by the watch and interrogated. The following day, he would be tried by municipal government officers.

In Barkor Street, there are a number of shrines to supposedly protective deities. Among the many such deities, the most popular are the gods of birth, who are thought to respectively protect those who are born in a particular year; the others are the gods of the land, who perform the same office for the place in which one is domiciled.

Another interesting thing about Barkor Street was how news was spread. News and comments were usually couched in negative rather than positive terms, that is, by means of satirical or political ballads. The targets were mostly political affairs, rulers, celebrities and so on. The way such news was passed from mouth to mouth was rather peculiar. For instance, on the morning of the first day of the first month by the Tibetan calendar, village women from the suburbs would come to fetch a bucket of "sacred water" from a well in Lhasa. There, they learned a new song, said to have been taught to them by Pelden Lhamo, a deity protecting the city. In this way, satirical ballads began to circulate, and would soon be on everybody's lips. The actual ballad composer did not make himself known. Every notable event resulted in a satirical song. Some even seemed to be of a prophetic nature, because they appeared before an event took place. Collections of such ballads are being compiled, in the hope of shedding new light on the modern history of Tibet using unofficial sources.

Starting in 1912, the government of Tibet began to mint copper coins and print paper notes. The copper coins came in 2.5 cent, 5 cent, 7.5 cent and 10 cent denominations. The silver coins contained 1.5 taels and 3 taels of silver, respectively. This picture is of a 5-cent copper coin.

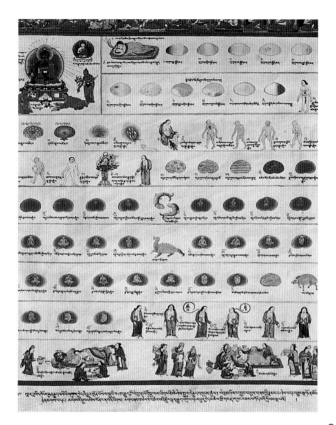

One of the paintings from the *Four Medical Classics* describing the formation of an embryo from the "fish period" to the "turtle period" to the "pig period," and finally to the "human period." *

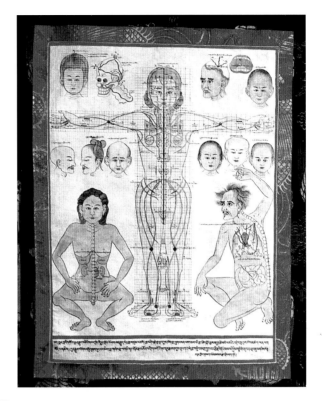

One of the paintings from the *Four Medical Classics*, showing the main and collateral channels of the human body.*

The life-sized statue of Sakyamuni at the age of 12 worshipped in the Jokhang Monastery. It is said to have been brought here by Princess Wencheng from the Tang Dynasty capital, Chang'an, in the 7th century. * (1956)

Thepungang blacksmiths at work. * (1957)

Monks engaged in business.* (1957)

Making wooden
bowls.

Business Center

Barkor Street is not only a religious center, it is also — perhaps even more so — a business center, a major market, and a commodity collecting and distributing center. The one-km-long street is lined with shops and stalls. From religious objects to daily necessities, commodities of all kinds and from all parts of the world are on display here. There is endless bargaining in this street. What is unique is that a seller's final price is called a "pledged price." This means that the seller makes a pledge to the Buddha that he is honest and it is the last price he can afford.

In the markets of old Lhasa, apart from tea, silk, porcelain, horse gear, spices, dried fruit and daily necessities, which came from the hinterland, most commodities came from abroad: coral, amber and diamonds from Europe; cloth, dyestuffs, bronze ware, pearls, per-

Removing surplus wool, the final stage in the making of a carpet. * (1957)

fume and medicines from Nepal; industrial articles such as aluminum pans from India; grain, sugar, musk and tobacco from Bhutan and Sikkim; and safflower and dried fruit from Ladakh. Tibetan products exported through Lhasa included gold, silver, salt, sheep's wool, woolen fabrics, carpets, medicines, fox skin, musk and borax. As can be seen, the imports were mostly finished products, whereas the exports were mostly raw materials. The export of sheep's wool, in particular, was considered the lifeline of the Tibetan economy. However, the wool had to be exported via India, which was ruled by Britain at that time, and Britain did not allow Tibet, on pain of embargo, to contact any other country to sell its wool. So Tibet was forced to sell its wool in India for Indian rupees. British and Indian merchants then re-sold the wool to other countries for handsome profits. This reminds one of robbers making

A folk singer carries on the tradition of singing songs with religious and historical themes. Hanging on the wall are Tangkas depicting such legends. *

profit by waylaying people.

The merchants of Barkor Street were mostly Tibetan, Han, Muslim and Nepalese. The Han Chinese were mostly from Beijing, and Yunnan, Sichuan and Qinghai provinces. The Yunnan merchants, in particular, were numerous, and had a long tradition of doing business in Tibet since the late 18th century. A contingent of merchants in the northwest of Yunnan was most active in this regard. Despite all hardships, they traveled between the Yunnan-Guizhou Plateau and the Qinghai-Tibet Plateau once a year bringing tea to Tibet. In return, they took local produce, hides and fur back to the hinterland. During the Anti-Japanese War (1937-1945), this route, known as the "ancient tea and horse road," served as China's only land access to the Allies. The route became fairly busy during that period.

Mongolians in Lhasa.

There were more than 40 shops run by people from Yunnan in Lhasa in the old days. Most of them were concentrated in Jiri Lane, part of Barkor Street. During the mid- and late 19th century, there was a Yunnan Guild Hall there. Businessmen from Yunnan had a good reputation. They had close connections with both the Tibetan nobles and Tibetan merchants. They gave generous presents to the high commissioners and made large donations to the major monasteries.

Many of the Yunnan merchants learned to speak the Tibetan language, and some settled down in Tibet with Tibetan wives, although they already had families and properties in Yunnan. This led to many romances as well as tragedies. However, such things are rarely mentioned nowadays.

It has been quite a long time since Beijing people started to do business in Tibet. At first, they engaged mainly in long-distance transportation. By the 1930s, there were 30 to 40 shops in Barkor Street alone owned by Beijing natives. The owners usually lived in Beijing and were responsible for the purchase of goods, while the businesses in Lhasa were managed by their employees. The goods, primarily silk brocade, porcelain, jade objects, bronze wares, silk thread, and arts and crafts, which were very popular with Tibetans, were first transported to Tianjin and loaded on to ships which sailed down to Hong Kong and thence to Calcutta. From Calcutta, the goods were taken to Kalimpong, and thence to Lhasa by mules, yaks or donkeys — a journey of 20 days. The whole trip would take about three months. This was carried out two or three times a year. Brocade sold particularly well; it was used not only for

A potter and his tea pots and bowls. *

clothes but also for decorative purposes in monasteries. Silk threads were also very popular, because both Tibetan men and women liked to mix them into their pigtails, which would then be coiled up on the head.

The people of the Khams-pa branch of the Tibetans, living in western Sichuan and eastern Tibet traditionally engaged in business. The largest Khams-pa business in the early 20th century, run by a man named Pondatsang, had branches and offices in many cities both at home and abroad. It was he who funded the 13th Dalai Lama's sojourn in India in 1910. When the Dalai Lama returned, Pondatsang was given the monopoly on the export of sheep's wool for the whole of Tibet. By the 1930s, even monks began to realize what benefits business would bring them, and many of the senior monks, officials and aristocrats became more interested in trade than in the revenue from their estates.

The Anti-Japanese War (1937-1945) provided a good opportunity for the rapid development of trade in Tibet. During the early years of the war, east China and the southeastern coastal area fell in the hands of Japan, and export by sea became impossible. A few years later, the Japanese army cut off the transportation route between Yunnan and Myanmar. Shortages of goods became very acute in the southwest of China (the Chinese government had withdrawn to Chongqing, in Sichuan Province, at that time), and goods which China needed had to be brought in either by airplane on "the Over Hump Route" or along the traditional caravan route from India to Tibet, and then to the

Gold- and silversmiths' shops along both sides of Barkor Street.

hinterland. So Lhasa became a busy hub of commerce. Caravans of mules traveled from India to Lijiang, to Kangding and then to Chengdu, crossing the whole plateau and covering a distance of several thousand kilometers.

In 1945, when the news of victory in the Anti-Japanese War reached Lhasa, the merchants in Barkor Street were wild with joy. The Representative Office of the Republic of China in Lhasa organized merchants from the hinterland to parade in the street with lanterns in celebration, and borrowed Pondatsang's residence to stage performances for two days. The costumes and stage sets for the performances were all made in a hurry with money donated by merchants. Officials of the Gaxag government, nobles and their families were invited.

Following the cessation of hostilities, communications with the outside world from the hinterland by both land and sea were resumed, and the "ancient tea and horse route" became quiet once more, as did the Lhasa markets. In the 1950s, many Han merchants returned to the hinterland; only those who had families in Lhasa stayed behind. A few settled down in India or Nepal, and became Overseas Chinese.

An early photo taken in a Lhasa studio. The original caption was "A minor Tibetan official."

Shackled convicts
were allowed to beg in
the street in old Tibet. *
(1957)

Life in the Sacred City

I would very much like to know who the girl in this picture is. Perhaps she was the most popular singer, Chushur Yeshe Drolma, in Lhasa in the 1930s and 1940s. Several friends of mine have seen pictures of her in her later years, so no one is sure that this is the same girl.

Since ancient times, the population of Lhasa has included more transient than permanent residents. To support these many migrating people, as well as the many religious and secular elite of the city, a substantial service sector became indispensable. In this sector could be found people at the bottom of the society.

The law codes of ancient Tibet divided people into three classes, and each class comprised three ranks. The first class included aristocrats and upper-class monks. They were the ruling group. The second class included merchants, office workers, lower-class monks, and others. Merchants occasionally rose to upper-class status, usually when an impoverished upper-class family married a daughter to a wealthy merchant. The third class comprised manual laborers. Below those three classes, there were people known as *jianmin* (outcast groups), who can be classified into five categories, namely, blacksmiths, butchers, funeral caretakers, pottery makers and entertainers. Similar to these people in social status were fishermen, boatmen, hunters, masons, etc. This system of social classification seems to have been borrowed from India, as was Buddhism. People of low social status were not allowed to become monks or nuns. They were not even allowed to kowtow to a monastery. They were not allowed to eat at the same table with upper-class people or to use eating utensils used by members of the upper class. If such a person had to speak to an upper-class person, he had to stand outside the gate of the latter's resi-

Selling odds and ends.

A caravan men on its way to Tibet in the 1920s.

dence and address him from there. Marriage between members of the different classes was almost unheard of. The child of such a marriage would inherit the status of the lower-ranking parent. In the 1950s an aristocrat fell in love with the daughter of a blacksmith. Ostracized by his family and friends, he fled with his bride deep into the mountains. It was only after the Democratic Reform was enacted in Tibet six years later, in 1959, that they dared to return to Lhasa and a new life.

Craftsmen and artists who had no land or any other means of production lived by selling their skills. They were organized into guilds by the local government. The guild rules were strictly conservative, dictating that the shape and making of a product must follow a fixed pattern. Innovation was strictly forbidden. So articles either for religious or secular purposes remained the same for many centuries. Blacksmiths, goldsmiths and silversmiths mostly lived in Tepengang Lane, which crossed Barkor East. The status of goldsmith and silversmith was slightly higher than that of blacksmith, and they called themselves "whitesmiths." The pottery makers' guild was located in Barkor Street, while their workshops were mostly in Maizhokunggar. Their wares were produced specially for the government, including the green glazed pottery made specially for the Dalai Lama.

Though meat was a staple food for everybody, including monks, in Tibet, butchers were especially discriminated against, probably because of the Buddhist distaste for the taking of life. In the old days, meat stalls were concentrated on Barkor North and East. The stalls on Barkor North were run by herdsmen from northern Tibet, while the stalls on Barkor East were managed by Muslims. Over the years, the Barkor East butchers piled up the horns of yaks they had slaughtered to make a wall. This strange wall still remains today.

Entertainers were regarded as little more than beggars in old Tibet, although a few outstanding singers were summoned to perform for the aristocrats. A noted street dancer called Sogda Yagu emerged in the 1940s. Particularly good at tap dance, he was able to dance to any song, be it English or Indian, with typical Tibetan-styled dancing movements. Despite his popularity with ordinary people, he lived in poverty. At night, he found shelter under bridges or huddled up together with the homeless and stray dogs at the foot of the West Pagoda on Barkor North. Following the Democratic Reform, he was given an apartment and some property. However, he continued to dance in the streets. In the 1990s, he was still often seen dancing in the streets to the accompaniment of pop songs played on a tape-recorder slung around his neck. He once appeared on a local TV program. He said proudly that he was "one of Lhasa's little decorations."

Book stalls in Barkor Street. The horizontal scrolls were block-printed. * (1956)

At the Shoton Festival in summer, eight Tibetan opera troupes were designated by the local government to come to Lhasa to give performances. As usual in this stagnant society, the programs were all fixed and supervised by a censorship body. A troupe could be banned for half a year or fined if it changed any of the words of the traditional songs. The best-known singer of the time of the 13th Dalai Lama, also his favorite, was Migmar Gyeltsen. It was said that when he sang in the Norbu Lingka, his voice could be heard at the foot of the Potala Place, one kilometer away. When he sang in the mansion of a noble, his resonant voice made the window paper quiver, or even crack. Yet this brilliant performer was kept on the lowest rung of the social ladder. One day in the 1940s, he dropped dead by the roadside on his way

Caravan men and their goods. This photo was probably taken in the 1920s or 1930s.

back from giving a performance at the Reting Monastery on the occasion of the Cuckoo Festival. His remains were chopped up and fed to the vultures on the Beggars' Celestial Burial Terrace. Many yeas have passed, but his name and stories about him are still familiar to the Tibetan people.

Serfs ruined by high rents and usury often fled to Lhasa, and settled in beggars' villages. The photo shows a corner of such a village. * (1957)

Beggars Bullied Beggars

In the past, the first thing a person coming to Lhasa noticed was the large numbers of beggars and dogs in the streets. Two rows of huts were built to give shelter to beggars at the end of Barkor Street, in front of the present-day Tibet Hospital. Lines of blind beggars linked together by a rope would be led by a dim-sighted beggar, chanting something religious and singing in deep and low voices. Monks would sit along the street cross-legged, chanting sutras and begging for alms. In front of each would be a long horizontal piece of cloth with quotations from the Buddhist scriptures written on theme. The most active were child beggars. Their begging songs were almost joyful. Their targets were usually wealthy ladies or girls. Their chants went something like:

What good looks you have, sister,
What a kind heart you have, sister,
Slim as a bamboo,
Fair as the moon.
... ...

Sister is going to give,
And the little beggar will soon get....

In a Buddhist society, it is considered meritorious to give alms, and the child beggars could almost always get something. The sight of pilgrims begging

Rowing ox-hide rafts on the Dragon King Pool in Lhasa at the Sakadawa Festival. * (1957)

Beggar-singers in the street.

their way to their destinations is common. Even the rich monasteries would send monks out to ask for alms. As this is still the practice in Tibet, tourists may sometimes find themselves being pestered by beggars.

The 15th day of the fourth month by the Tibetan calendar is the Sakadawa Festival, the traditional date on which Sakyamuni was born, became enlightened and died. It is the most important religious festival in Tibet, and is also known as the Poor People's Festival. On that day, beggars from all over Tibet congregate

This blind old beggar was seen in Lhasa for many years. * (1956)

around the Potala Palace, waiting for alms.

What is different about begging in Tibet from that in other parts of the world is that beggars often give change. If you give a beggar a ten-yuan note and say that you want nine yuan in change, he will give it to you. In monasteries too, if one wants to donate ten yuan but all one has is a one-hundred yuan note, it is quite all right to pick up ninety yuan from the pile of money in front of the statue of Buddha.

Half a century ago, among the beggars in Lhasa, especially along Barkor South where the prison was located, was a special group who were shackled with wooden or iron fetters. If the shackles were chains, the beggar could move around, but if they were made of iron or wooden plates, the beggar could hardly move. They stood or sat on the ground, begging for money. They were either offenders being paraded in public or people convicted of minor crimes. Senior beggars would be appointed to supervise prisoners begging in street —- a way to reduce the pressures of supplying the prison.

Ngantsesha, on Barkor South, was responsible for public security in Lhasa. It always had a very small staff, and relied upon an organization named Rokyepa, made up of so-called senior beggars, to help maintain order and see to the upkeep of sanitary

Shackles for convicts. * (1957)

This kind of shackle was used for convicts who had committed serious crimes. *

work in the city. This organization was said to have appeared as early as when Lhasa came into being. In the early days, the Lhasa River was very close to the city, which was threatened by floods every summer. King Songtsan Gampo organized a group of captives, beggars, vagabonds and convicted criminals to build and maintain the river's dykes. As time went by, they formed an organization of their own, the members of which were only allowed to marry either within the group or with people from other *jianmin* groups, such as blacksmiths and butchers. A thousand years later, this organization still existed. It was classified into different ranks. Those at the lowest level might climb up the ranks, but those at the top of this organization were unable to get out of it.

The head of the Rokyepa was appointed by the government, and was allowed to wear a round hat and a gold earring, indicating his status as a minor official. Later, the riverbed of the Lhasa River moved south, and there was no longer any need for a special contingent to maintain the dykes. Consequently, the Rokyepa was given the responsibility for flogging and torturing convicts, supervising beggars, removing corpses from the street and the changing of Buddhist streamers in front of the Jokhang Monastery and the Norbu Lingka just before New Year. The Rokyepa constables earned no salary; their income came from graft and begging.

Since they owned nothing, they had no fear of losing anything. They were a group of lawless people. They seemed to have no fear of the aristocrats and high-ranking officials. Whenever they heard the news of a ceremony, either for a wedding, a funeral or a promotion, held by an elite family, they would swarm to the residence concerned, where the host had to treat them with food and drink, and give them the sum of money they requested. If they were not satisfied, they would make a terrifying "Ahhhh…" sound in chorus. It was believed that such a noise would summon an evil spirit which would harass the host family. After they had left, their wives and children would arrive and repeat the performance. As if that wasn't enough, the visit by the wives and children would be followed by one by ordinary beggars.

The Rokyepa ruffians regularly blackmailed peasants and herdsmen who

A scorpion pit, into which convicts were thrown in the old days.

The chopping off of arms and the gouging out of eyes were common penalties for crimes in old Tibet. Both the 13th and 14th Dalai Lamas promulgated decrees abolishing such cruel punishments.

came from countryside to Lhasa to sell their produce. In such a harsh society, the poor had no sympathy for the poor, and beggars bullied other beggars.

The Rokyepa was dissolved during the Democratic Reform of 1959.

On the occasion of the Shoton Festival in summer, 12 Tibetan opera troupes would be invited to give performances before the Dalai Lama in the Norbu Lingka. *

Chapter 4
The High Commissioners and the Historical Archives of the Republic of China

導俗洵治世之良規熟

生為行持之

呼圖克圖妙契玄微廣窮

扇宗風於寶樹化溥烏

自於珠林德弘

The office of the high commissioners of the Qing Court in Lhasa. *

This picture, taken in the 1920s, shows You Tai (third from the left), who served as the high commissioner of the Qing Court in Tibet from the 28th year to the 32nd year (1902-1906) of the reign of Emperor Guangxu. He was later dismissed and punished for engaging in graft and other irregularities. *

The office of the high commissioners was located to the west of the Jokhang Monastery.

Lord Zhang from the Sea

From the sea came Lord Zhang
Who brought happiness and peace to Tibet.
— from a Tibetan ballad

Even today, whenever the name Zhang Yintang is mentioned to Tibetans their eyes light up in admiration and fondness. As well as the ballad about him, Zhang is commemorated in the name of a popular flower in Tibet, the "Lord Zhang Flower," which can often be seen in residential courtyards and public places in Lhasa. The plant grows chest-high, and has eight petals either red or white. If you look closely, the red can be further divided into pink and purple. It blossoms in August and September. Its formal name is coreopsis, and some Han Chinese call it the "eight-petal plum." In Lhasa, there is a Lord Zhang Vegetable Garden and a

From 1727, the Qing Court regularly sent a resident high commissioner to administer Tibetan affairs on behalf of the Central Government. This photo was taken in the early 1920s. *

Lord Zhang Tree. Moreover, a kind of hat with a rolled-up brim is called a "Zhang hat," since Zhang Yintang once wore such a hat.

Zhang Yintang was sent to Tibet by the Qing Court in connection with Britain's invasion of Tibet in 1904. At the end of that year, the Qing repudiated the so-called Lhasa Convention, which the invaders had forced the Tibetan government to sign, and sent Tang Shaoyi and Zhang Yintang to Calcutta with the aim of changing the contents of the Convention. The negotiations broke down in October 1905. Fully cognizant of Britain's ambition to seize control of Tibet, as well as of Tibet's weakness, Zhang proposed to reform the administrative and social systems there. With the approval of the Qing government, Zhang was sent to Tibet to carry out his planned reforms. Since he traveled by sea to India before going overland from there to Tibet, he was called "Lord Zhang from the sea."

Zhang went to Tibet in the capacity of imperial envoy. It was the first time that a Han had been assigned such a mission; for the previous 200 years, all the high commissioners sent to Tibet had been either Manchus or Mongols. Zhang was born in Nanhai, Guangdong Province. He had been a *juren*, a successful candidate in the imperial examination at the provincial level. When he was young, he served as an attaché and a general consul in the United States, and was much influenced by advanced bourgeois thinking of the time. An enter-

Colonel Young-husband and the high commissioner meet at a horse race. This photo was taken by a member of Younghusband's invasion force in 1904.

The Guan Di Temple was built with donations from General Fu Kang'an and his subordinates after the victory over the Korga. The temple stands on Mill Mountain, to the southwest of the Potala Palace. It is a typical Han-style structure. The photo shows the temple in a dilapidated state.

prising person, he was determined to put his new ideas into practice in Tibet. Unfortunately, given the differences in social conditions and political structures in the hinterland and Tibet, his reforms made little headway.

A stone stele in the Guan Di Temple, bearing an inscription by General Fu Kang'an, recounting the victory over the Korga invaders.

The first thing Zhang did after arriving in Lhasa was to have High Commissioner You Tai and some other Qing officials stationed in Tibet dismissed for corruption and collusion with foreign powers. Approved by the Qing government, this was a very popular step among the local people. Zhang then made 19 proposals in respect of the administration of Tibet and 24 provisions for settling unsolved problems. The key to this systematic reform program lay in reform of the political system, that is, separation of religion and politics. He suggested that grand titles and generous stipends be given to the Dalai Lama and the Panchen Lama, while at the same time limiting their administrative powers to cover religious affairs only. He wanted to increase the power of the Central Government over Tibet by establishing the position of chief administrator to replace the high commissioner. Due to the complicated circumstances of the time, only a few of Zhang's reforms were carried through. But these were important and lasting ones; for instance, nine departments were set up in charge of internal and external affairs, military training, finance, education, the police and justice, industry and commerce, roads and mines, salt and tea, and agriculture. Of these, four departments continued to function until the Democratic Reform of 1959.

Zhang's proposals for reform of the military system included compulsory recruitment instead of enlisting only men who owned a certain amount of land, dispatching military instructors from the hinterland, and setting up a military academy and munitions factory in Lhasa. In the field of economic reform, he urged better use of natural advantages, the development of local industry and the sending of students abroad to study technology and manufacturing. Zhang also encouraged the improvement of road communications with neighboring countries, land reclamation, and the development of mining, trade and enterprises, using preferential tax policies. His most revolutionary proposal, however, was perhaps the one to get monks to engage in useful work instead of just sitting around chanting sutras all day and begging.

He strongly urged the establishment of an educa-

A portrait of Madame Liu Manqing. She was born in 1906 in Lhasa. Her father was a Han and her mother a Tibetan. She graduated from Beijing National Normal College, and was fluent in both the Tibetan and Chinese languages. She once served as an official in the government of the Republic of China. In 1929, she was sent to Lhasa as an envoy by the Central Government, and met the 13th Dalai Lama twice.

tion department and the opening of more schools, and even free schooling for children. He called on the monasteries to run schools and adopt modern curricula.... However, all these were but fond dreams. First, the coffers of the Qing were empty, and, second, the monks were against education for lay people, especially those of the lower classes. This is not surprising, for it was precisely by keeping the people ignorant that the monks could exercise their despotic authority.

Zhang Yintang also failed to change the backward social habits of the Tibetans. He had two pamphlets, titled *Elementary Ethics* and *Change Your Habits and Ways*, published. These pamphlets advocated humanism, hygiene, good manners, a scientific way of life, etc. But Tibet's strictly conservative and hierarchical society proved too hard a nut to crack.

From generation to generation, the people of Lhasa have passed down the story of how Zhang called all the officials, secular and clerical, to the meeting hall of the Jokhang Monastery, and gave them lectures on the natural laws of evolution, "survival of the fittest," and the necessity of reform to improve Tibetan society. By giving examples of Britain's colonization and control of neighboring India, Sikkim and Bhutan, he called on the local people to strive to make Tibet strong, and woke them up to realize that Tibet was backward. The influence of his ideas was long lasting, as 20 years later, the 13th Dalai Lama instituted new and progressive

Madame Liu Manqing poses with monks.

policies, such as sending students abroad to study and establishing a modern military force. He was very likely enlightened by Zhang Yintang's lectures. Also, in line with Zhang Yintang's ideas for enlightening the people of Tibet, Lian Yu, the last high commissioner, published a newspaper using both Tibetan and vernacular Chinese, which further stirred interest in reform.

Carvings on the cliff face of Chakpori Hill,

The Tibetan aristocracy was the main stumbling block to reform. As long as they ruled Tibet as a place of feudal serfdom under a despotic theocracy, no reform could be thoroughgoing. Further opposition came from the Qing Court itself, where both Han and Manchu officials were alarmed at and resented Zhang Yintang's punishment of corrupt officials in Tibet. Zhang's eagerness to press forward with reform caused mistakes that gave his opponents something to use against him. They started a campaign of slander against Zhang. As rumors and complaints kept entering the emperor's ears, this patriotic and royal official was removed from his post and sent to conduct commercial negotiations in India. Thus this "Lord Zhang from the sea route" went back by sea. His seven-month hard work day and night in Tibet left him coughing up blood. Before he left, he donated his personal property — 50 taels (one tael equals 31.25 g) of gold and 50 taels of silver – for the promotion of education in Tibet.

Tibetans used to stick out their tongues as a polite gesture of welcome. Zhang Yingtang advocated abolishing this practice.

Strangely, no photo of Zhang Yintang can be found, while there is a stack of photos of the rascally

Today, only in remote places is the custom of sticking out the tongue as a greeting still practiced.

You Tai. They were taken by Britons. In the Tibet Archives, I once saw a document concerning forestation submitted by monk and lay officials of the agriculture department to Zhang Yintang. It was something he must have seen. It says: "At the order of Your Highness, it is planned to plant trees in the suburbs of Lhasa and turn more than twenty *lingka* in the city proper into public parks. Besides, tea bushes are to be planted in the eastern area." But after Zhang had to leave office the plan for public parks fell through, and the funds allocated for tree planting leaked away. The Agriculture Department had been granted 1000 taels of silver (10,000 Tibetan yuan) for employing workers to plant trees along the road from Lhasa to Gyantse. But in actual fact, the work was contracted to a local foreman with a payment of 600 to 700 Tibetan yuan. The work of tree planting was sporadic, and those trees that were planted were hardly up to standard. Besides, there was no plan to care for the trees after planting.

Zhang Yintang did a great deal within the short period of seven months that he was in office in Tibet. His influence, which is unable to be measured, was long lasting. His ability, personal charisma and his integrity earned him the reputation of a hero in China. He is no doubt still a model for those Han Chinese who go to work in Tibet. His spirit will be remembered forever by both the Tibetan and Han peoples.

A portrait of Huang Musong, who went to attend the funeral of the 13th Dalai Lama on behalf of the Central Government. *

Chen Xizhang, one-
time head of the Tibet
Office of the Republic
of China, and his
wife. *

A Thousand Years of
Turbulent Relations

Old Lhasa witnessed stormy years in the first half
of the 20th century. The lamaist state, beset with difficulties both internally and externally, was tottering.

Following the fall of the Qing Dynasty, China went
through a period of upheaval. The Republic of China
was established in 1911. But for almost 40 years —
from 1911 to 1949 – there was nationwide turmoil. First
of all, there was the period of warlord rule. Then the
Guomintang (Nationalists) and the Communists coop-
erated and split on two occasions. Then there was the
Anti-Japanese War, the Liberation War…. The social
order was totally disrupted. The relationship between
Tibet and the Central Government lapsed into the most
abnormal period since the Yuan Dynasty.

Housed in the Tibet Archives today are 600,000 to
700,000 documents and objects, of which a large num-

ber record exchanges between the Tibetan government and the Central Government of the Republic of China from 1911. They do not include those kept in the Nanjing Historical Archives. They indicate that the government of the Republic of China did its utmost over several decades to exercise its sovereignty over Tibet despite all difficulties. It endeavored to save Tibet from being split from China and becoming a colony of Britain.

For the sake of state sovereignty and national unity, the Guomintang and the Communists put aside their political differences, and upheld the banner of national sovereignty which had been handed down for a thousand years. The period of the Republic of China was short, but it accomplished a few things of great significance concerning Tibet. For instance, it restored the title to the 13th Dalai Lama, who had been removed by the last emperor of the Qing Dynasty. When the 13th Dalai Lama died, the government of the Republic of China sent Huang Musong to attend his funeral in Lhasa and restored the title to him posthumously. At the same time, the Tibet Office of the Republic of China

After the 13th Dalai Lama passed away in 1934, the government of the Republic of China sent Huang Musong, deputy chief of the General Staff, to represent it at the funeral. The picture shows Tibetans carrying Guomindang (Nationalist Party) and Republic of China flags, waiting to welcome Huang. *

Madame Liu Manqing arrives in Lhasa.

was established. The Central Government was also involved in the confirmation and enthronement of the 14th Dalai Lama. Wu Zhongxin was sent to attend the enthronement ceremony on behalf of the Central Government of the Republic of China. Tibet also had offices of the Dalai and Panchen Lamas set up in Nanjing, capital of the Republic of China, at that time. Delegates from Tibet also attended the National Assembly. One major responsibility of those offices was to arrange accommodation for Tibetan officials visiting Nanjing.

This is the document by which the government of the Republic of China granted the 13th Dalai Lama the posthumous title of Great Master of Patriotism, Magnanimity, Benevolence and Sagacity. *

Before Huang Musong took office in Tibet, several groups of representatives of the Central Government had visited Tibet since 1919. One of them was a lady named Liu Manqing. Entrusted by Chiang Kai-shek, she went to Tibet as a non-official representative in 1930. The 13th Dalai Lama, in an unprecedented move,

The ninth Panchen Lama presides over a memorial ceremony for the 13th Dalai Lama.

On July 1, 1928, the government of the Republic of China granted the 13th Dalai Lama the title of Great Master of Patriotism, Magnanimity, Benevolence and Sagacity.

This is the decree issued by the Executive *Yuan* recognizing the "soul boy" Lhamo Dondrup of Qinghai Province as the 14th Dalai Lama, and allocating 400,000 *yuan* for the enthronement ceremony. *

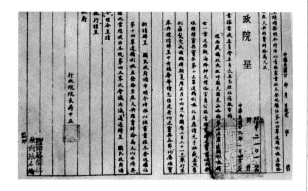

Wu Zhongxin, chairman of the Commission for Mongolian and Tibetan Affairs of the government of the Republic of China, was sent to Lhasa to preside over the confirmation and enthronement ceremonies for the new Dalai Lama. He arrived in Lhasa on January 15, 1940, and was warmly welcomed by Tibetans both clerical and lay at the Official-Receiving Pavilion in the western suburbs of Lhasa. *

received her in person. He told her that he would not be enticed by the British, and that his heart was with China. Liu later wrote a book titled, *My Mission to Xikang and Tibet.*

Huang Musong broke the ice between the Tibetan and Han peoples during his trip to Tibet in 1934 to deliver a memorial speech at the funeral of the 13th Dalai Lama. Instead of going there by the traditional sea route via India, he traveled along the Sichuan-Tibet route. For one thing, he wanted to avoid any obstruction by Britain, and for another, he wanted to investigate the disputed border between Xikang and Tibet. His mission involved restoring the title to the late Dalai Lama, delivering a memorial speech at the ceremony, and presenting gifts to officials and alms to monasteries. His major aim was to restore the relations between the Central Government and the local government of Tibet. The Gaxag government, including both monk and lay officials, convened the Tsongdu (People's Conference), and sent a letter to the Central Government stipulating 10 provisions, which included recognizing that Tibet was part of China and subject to the rule of the Central Government and consenting to the stationing of representatives of the Central Government in Lhasa. Before Huang left for Nanjing, he established a representative office, an observatory and a radio transmitter in Tibet.

One of the unsuccessful candidates for the title of "soul boy."

Upon his return to Nanjing, he was appointed chairman of the Commission for Mongolian and Tibetan Affairs. The Lhasa representative office, observatory, radio and Lhasa Primary School (which was opened by the Central Government later) operated until 1951, when Tibet was peacefully liberated.

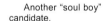

Another "soul boy" candidate.

The reincarnation ("soul boy") of the Dalai Lama, Tenzin Gyatso, was supposed to have occurred in a peasant family in Qijiachuan (Taktser), Huangzhong County, Qinghai Province, in 1935, when Tenzin Gyatso was identified as the soul boy by the government of the Republic of China, at the request of the local government of Tibet. The Central Government ordered Ma Bufang, warlord of Qinghai, to send

In February 1940, Wu Zhongxin presided over the enthronement ceremony for the 14th Dalai Lama in the Potala Palace. *

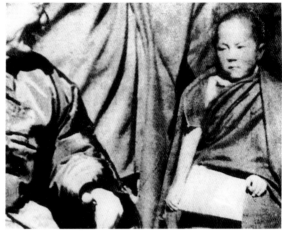

The 14th Dalai Lama at the enthronement ceremony.*

troops to escort the boy to Tibet, at a cost of 100,000 yuan. To manifest its sovereignty and to follow historical tradition, the Nanjing government also sent Wu Zhongxin, chairman of the Mongolian and Tibetan Affairs Commission, to preside over the confirmation and enthronement ceremonies. On February 5, 1940, the government of the Republic of China issued an order announcing that Tenzin Gyatso was the 14th Dalai Lama, and allocated 400,000 yuan for the enthronement ceremony. On February 22, 1940, Wu Zhongxin presided over the enthronement ceremony, held in the Potala Palace, on behalf of the Central Government of the Republic of China. Britain, which at that time was seeking to wrest Tibet from China, also sent a delegation to offer congratulations, but the government of Tibet made an appropriate arrangement which clearly

It was here, in the Lotus Pavilion in the Norbu Lingka, that Wu Zhongxin examined the 14th Dalai Lama. *

In 1931, the ninth Panchen Lama attended the National Assembly.

indicated that Tibet was an inalienable part of China.

For decades, to be united with or split from China has been an issue of great concern with the ruling elite of Tibet. It hesitated, finding it difficult to determine its own position. It was true that there was a separatist force. But how could the long-standing political and economic ties between Tibet and the hinterland be severed as simply as that? What benefit could Tibet get from independence? Throughout history, every time communications between Tibet and the hinterland were interrupted, the Tibetans suffered. Take tea, for example. Tea has long been indispensable to the Tibetan people. Aristocrats, high-ranking officials and commoners all drank tea. Tibet produces no tea at all,

The staff members of the Tibet Office of the Republic of China with merchants from Yunnan. The head of the office was Chen Xizhang (sixth from the right, front row).

and so if the route to the hinterland was blocked the supply of tea was reduced, and its price would immediately rise.

The economy, the foundation of a society, is something the rulers could not afford to neglect. During the second expulsion of Han people from Tibet in 1949, only those related to politics were expelled,

In 1934, the ninth Panchen Lama was carried in a sedan-chair with a yellow silk canopy to the Buddhist assembly for the worship of Kalachakra.

such as the staff working in the Tibet Office of the Central Government and secret agents of the Kuomintang, and not Han traders. The Han merchants shut their stores in Barkor Street for only a few days and then reopened to resume their businesses.

From the time of Huang Musong's 1934 mission to 1949, only the Tibet Office of the Central Government represented the Republic of China. The directors of the Office in this period were Kong Qingzong and Shen Zonglian. An acting director stayed on until the last minute. The staff included Li Youyi, a scholar, and English interpreter Liu Shengqi.

In June 1934, the ninth Panchen Lama offered blessings to the residents of Shanghai by chanting Buddhist sutras through a megaphone.

Apart from them, there were groups of Kuomintang secret agents. Compared with the high commissioners sent by the Qing Court, their position and power were far inferior.

In 1947, the government of Tibet, headed by Taktra Rimpoche, executed Living

After the 13th Dalai Lama passed away in 1933, the next year the government of the Republic of China held a memorial meeting at the Examination *Yuan* in Nanjing. The picture shows the archway erected for the occasion.

Buddha Reting for the crime of being "pro-Han." After that, Lhasa was in a white terror. Those who had been close to the Tibet Office of the Central Government had to stay away. At the same time, the Kuomintang itself was on the verge of collapse. All those working for Kuomintang were on tenterhooks. Nevertheless, it managed to keep a presence in Lhasa until it was driven from the mainland in 1949.

In retrospect, no matter how little the Tibet Office of the Central Government could achieve, its mere existence had significance. Unfortunately, the Kuomintang government was fully occupied in the battles against Japan externally and against the Communists internally. It was too busy to take care of Tibet. Its reaction to the positive attitudes of the Tibetan government was slow or even indifferent. Its instructions to the Tibet Office was "to make no error is a

淨妙莊嚴

Interior of the
memorial hall.

A photo taken after
the ninth Panchen
Lama paid homage at
the memorial service.

great achievement; to take no move is a great merit." Such a policy made the staff unable to do anything significant. Many of them wrote memoirs describing life of that period.

It was also in this period that the Dalai Lama and Panchen Lama set up their respective offices in Nanjing, capital of the Republic of China. In 1923, the ninth Panchen Lama, complaining of a sudden huge increase in military expenditure and exorbitant taxes in Tibet created by the Dalai Lama, left Tibet for the hinterland. There he spent the last 14 years of his life. He prayed for the prosperity of the motherland, made generous donations for the War of Resistance Against the Japanese Aggression. He enjoyed high esteem among the

The government of the Republic of China conferred the title Great Master Defender of the Nation and Propagator of the Doctrine Hutuktu on Regent Radreng in 1934. The photo shows the edict and the seal. *

Chinese people. In 1937, when he was on his way back to Tibet, he died in Yushu in Qinghai Province. A massive funeral ceremony was held for him by the Central Government.

In 1949, the enthronement of the 10th Panchen Lama was held in the Kumbum Monastery in Qinghai. He lived there until December 1951, when he left for Tibet.

In the spring of 1959, the 10th Panchen Lama came to the Jokhang Monastery and gave a speech to a large number of monks.*

The 10th Panchen Lama prayed at the Tashilhunpo Monastery in 1957. *

Chapter 5

The Last Days of the
Rule of the Divine King

British invaders entering Lhasa in August 1904.

The representatives who attended the Simla Conference. British representative McMahon is in the center of the front row; Chinese representative Chen Yifan is third from the left in the front row; the Tibetan representative is third from the right in the front row. This is the only photo we could find of the Simla Conference. There are a number of photos available showing the British invaders in Lhasa, which were taken by the invaders themselves. *

Dawa Dondrup, who took part in the resistance to the British invaders in 1904. In 1963, when he was 83 years old, he told children about the fight to oppose British aggression against Tibet. He was a peasant living in Kangma County. *

Internal Dissension Invites Outside Bullying

The return of Hong Kong and Macao to China marked the end of the colonial period in Asia. But not every Chinese knows that the shadow of colonization still exists in southeastern Tibet and the border area of western Tibet. There are still borders to be demarcated, disputes over territory. Such disputes, which have even resulted in armed clashes, have all been caused essentially by the British colonialists and their successors.

The so-called McMahon Line is an unhealed wound in the flesh of China. The semi-tropical area and the mountainous tropical area to the south of the high ridge of the Himalayas, namely, Lower Zayü (Gyigang), Lhoyü and Monyü have been part of Tibet since ancient times. China's sovereignty over those areas is indisputable. In Monyü, the Raksasi Temple has been a place of annual sacrifice for Tibetan officials for centuries, and in the area of Lhoyü there is a hill known as the Magic Hill, which is a sacred place for believers in the indigenous Tibetan religion known as Bon. Every 12 years, that is, the Year of the Monkey by the traditional Tibetan calendar, Bon adherents go to walk round the hill.

This area covers 90,000 sq km, a size similar to that of Zhejiang Province. It has a total population of 100,000 Monba, Lhoba and Tibetan people. To its east lies the largest chasm in the world — the Yarlung Zangbo Canyon — in the south of Medog County. On both sides of the lower reaches of the Yarlung Zangbo River and the vast area between the river to Moindawang in the west are endless snow-

Defensive wall to the north of Tüna built before the war.

The final meeting between the Da-dpon (senior military official) and Francis Young-husband. *

Before the British army invaded Tibet, Francis Younghusband had this photo taken in Darjeeling. On the way to Lhasa, he and his army killed several thousand Tibetans.

capped mountains, thick forests and fertile farmland. The sixth Dalai Lama Tsangyang Gyatso, who was also a great poet, was born in Moindawang, the administrative center of the Monyü area. A decree was issued by the Tibetan government that his clan would have permanent ownership of its land, serfs and properties, and be exempted from corvee labor. The inhabitants of the Monyü area were mostly government laborers and serfs, while some were owned by Lhasa aristocrats, and others by the three leading monasteries, which owned land and temples everywhere in Tibet.

How could a place the sovereignty of which is indisputable become an area of dispute? To explain this, we have to start from the Simla Conference. The situation in China in 1913 was rather complex. The British government took advantage of the anxiety of Yuan Shikai, a northern warlord, to be recognized by Britain as the new ruler of China to force the Chinese government to participate in a meeting held in Simla, India. The conference agenda included no Sino-Indian border issues, but the border disputes between Tibet and Han-inhabited areas, a totally internal issue of China. Six months before the conference, Britain sent Charles Bell to Chomo, where he met privately with Silon Shatra Paljor Dorje, a temporary official of the local government of Tibet who was to attend the conference. After three months of conspiratorial talks, they struck a political deal. Their strategy was that the representative of Tibet to the conference would raise the issue of a "greater Tibet." Then the British delegate, McMahon, would introduce a pre-arranged "compromise." Step by step, they pursued the "independence of Tibet." So, at the beginning of the conference, Xazha raised a six-point proposal demanding territory from Sichuan,

After the British army entered Gyantse, the Tibetan soldiers, with Gyantse Fortress as their base, used gunpowder, knives, spears and even stones to fight the invaders. The picture shows the fortress. *

The British army bombarded a village in Gyantse in the summer of 1904, causing a large number of civilian casualties. *

Yunnan, Qinghai, Gansu and Tibet, which was obviously not within the jurisdiction of the local government of Tibet. This was, of course, rejected. Chen Yifan, the delegate of the Chinese government, put forward a seven-point program to solve the dispute between Tibet and the Han-inhabited areas. As it was a stalemate, McMahon fished out the "compromise," which provided that Tibet would be divided into an "Inner Tibet" and an "Outer Tibet." "Outer Tibet" referred to Tibet under the control of the local government of Tibet, while "Inner Tibet" referred to adjacent regions inhabited by Tibetans, Han and other ethnic groups. According to this plan, "Outer Tibet" could exercise autonomy for the time being. The British delegate used a blue pencil to draw a line between so-called "Inner Tibet" and "Outer Tibet," and then used a red pencil to draw another line along the south of "Outer Tibet." No one paid much attention to the red line, focusing instead on the blue line. The demand for an "Inner Tibet" and an "Outer Tibet" was strongly opposed by the Chinese people. Chen Yifan refused to sign the agreement, and the Chinese government, headed by Yuan Shikai, had to announce that the agreement was null and void. Britain and Tibet privately signed the agreement, but it was stated in this agreement that it would have no effect without China's acknowledgement. So the so-called Simla Agreement was a mere piece of waste paper.

In 1935, a British botanist crossed the border to do

some research and was arrested by the Tibet government. To solve the problem of whether the botanist had crossed the border or not, the Indian government searched for some past documents and happened to find the drawing with blue and red lines. Indians were delighted, yet dared not use it since that document itself was invalid. Stealthily, they withdrew and destroyed all copies of the 1929 edition of the *Acheson Collection of Treaties* which carried that Silam Agreement. Instead, they published a new edition but with the same old publishing date. At the same time, the British government of India began surveying the border region in preparation for its annexation, setting up tax collection offices there. In 1951, when China was busy fighting the USA invaders in Korea, the newly independent Indian government took the opportunity to occupy Moindawang. In 1959, Indian troops started to move north of the "McMahon Line," and in 1962, clashes between them and Chinese troops resulted in the Indians being driven back. Then the Chinese troops returned back to the north of the red line. It was another 10 years before China and India resumed diplomatic relations, but to this day the border issue remains unsolved.

As the old saying goes, "Internal dissension invites outside bullying." The 13th Dalai Lama unscrupulously let the wolf in through the door to solve the disputes between Tibetan and Han residents of Tibet. Interference by Britain complicated the contradictions between nationalities in China. Official documents which have only come to light in recent years in Britain, the United States and India fully expose the plot to split Tibet from China and put it under their "protection."

In March 1904 alone, the British army killed more than 1,400 Tibetans. This picture of Tibetan captives was taken by a British soldier. *

The four Kalons who were involved in the conclusion of the *Treaty of Lhasa* in 1904.

After Britain established the East India Company, a base of aggression, in Bengal in the 17th century, it began a series of aggressive expansion moves into South Asia. When it had full control of India, it advanced northward. In the early 19th century, it gradually took control of the southern foothills of the Himalayas. Sikkim lay in its way. This small country had been a dependency of Tibet since ancient times, and when it was invaded by the British army in 1888, it asked the Qing court for help. But, having just been defeated by the allied armies of Britain and France, the Qing government was unable to give any assistance. The Gaxag government deployed its army at Mount Lungdo, but the British were victorious, and occupied the whole of Sikkim. Next, Bhutan and Nepal, which had for centuries had a very close relationship with Tibet, also fell into the hands of Britain. The next target of the British aggressors was Tibet. But as long as Tibet was part of China, Britain would have to consider its interests vis-a-vis China as a whole. To put Tibet under its "protection," Britain would have to find a way to split Tibet from China. That was the origin of the Simla Conference. This was the political situation of Tibet in the first half of the 20th century.

In the wake of the Simla Conference and the drawing of the illegal McMahon Line, step by step Britain and India expanded the area under their control, speeded up control over the ruling class of Tibet, and did their utmost to bring about Tibet's independence or so-called "de facto" independence. India, a colony itself, regarded itself as a semi-master of Tibet. When, in the mid-1940s, India declared independence, it still regarded itself as the protector of Tibet.

In face of such a complicated situation, rulers of Tibet including the 13th Dalai Lama inevitably had to embark on an arduous path and agonize over choices to determine how to keep the political and religious order in Tibet, and in which direction Tibet would go.

A picture of British officers taken after the occupation of Gyantse. *

Tupden Gyatso, the
13th Dalai Lama. *

A fresco in the Potala Palace showing Empress Dowager Cixi receiving the 13th Dalai Lama in Beijing in 1908.*

Where Would the Divine King Go?

The 13th Dalai Lama, the Divine King, was a symbol of the highest authority of both the temporal and the religious powers in Tibet. For centuries, the people of this snow-clad land of Tibet had been prostrate at the feet of the Dalai Monks, the super rulers who were believed to control one's life, both the present one and the ones to come. The 13th Dalai Lama himself became a legendary figure. He was born in a chaotic period, and had to face many challenges. He went in exile twice, and his title was removed twice.

The first time he went into exile was in 1904, when the British invaders approached Lhasa, and he was forced to leave. He went to Mongolia first, hoping that he would be supported by Russia against Britain. But the Russians were busy fighting a losing war with the Japanese. Then he had to turn to Beijing. Though the

The 13th Dalai Lama
seated on his throne.

Qing Court confirmed his title, it did no more to help
him. After more than four years in Mongolia, Qinghai,
Mount Wutai and Beijing, he returned to Lhasa, hu-
miliated and disappointed. To his dismay, he found
that Tibet was tightly controlled by High Commissioner
Lian Yu. With pain in his heart, he left Tibet again, this
time for India, where he asked Britain for political asylum.
But for fear of offending Russia and China and with
wider ambitions than simply seizing Tibet, the British
government replied expressly that it had no intention
of interfering in China's internal affairs.

The fall of the Qing Dynasty in 1911 provided a
good opportunity for the 13th Dalai Lama to return to
Tibet. At the time when he regained his power over
Tibet, China's hinterland was racked by warlord feuds,
and a dozen provinces had declared their

When the 5th Dalai Lama visited Beijing in 1652, Emperor Shunzhi met him and gave him a sedan-chair with a golden roof and yellow silk canopy as a gift. From then on, each Dalai Lama, after going through the enthronement ceremony with the approval of the emperor, was entitled to ride in this sedan-chair. The photo shows the 13th Dalai Lama in the sedan-chair.

independence. The Dalai Lama, having experienced exile and bitter experiences, made up his mind to promote new policies.

But all his reform measures clashed with traditional concepts and the current administrative system. Within 10 years, his new policies had fizzled out due to internal opposition. For instance, he wanted to expand the Tibetan army, but there was no money for this purpose. In the meantime, sharp differences between the Dalai and Panchen Lamas led to the latter leaving Tibet for the hinterland of China in 1923. Meanwhile, Charong, the commander-in-chief of the Tibetan army and his subordinate officers defied the Dalai Lama's order abolishing torture and savage punishments by chopping off the arm of one soldier and the leg of another for minor

A mandala made of strands of 200,000 pearls given to the 13th Dalai Lama as a gift by Empress Dowager Cixi. *

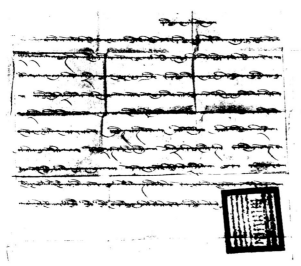

offences, and then paraded the victims in Barkor Street. For this, the Dalai Lama dismissed Charong from his post of commander-in-chief and then stripped him of the position of Kalon.

In the meantime, the traditional trade between the Ti-

In a memorial presented to Emperor Guangxu by the 13th Dalai Lama in 1908, the latter stated, "... for the teachings of Sakyamuni and consolidation of the territory of the emperor, I often chant sutras and pray...." *

betan and Han peoples had come almost to a halt, and the economy and trade of Tibet were controlled entirely by British India. Shoddy commodities from India flooded the markets of Lhasa, and Britain and India enjoyed all the privileges brought about by unequal treaties. They then began to interfere in the politics of Tibet.

We have no idea what was on the mind of the Dalai Lama during this period. But in the early 1920s he told Zhu Xiu, a representative of the Central Government, that he would not have turned to Britain had it not been for the high-handed treatment he had received from the high commissioners. In 1930, he told Liu Manqing, a woman employee of the Office of Civil Affairs, sent by the Central Government: "What I expect most of China is real unity and peace.... The British, indeed, have a mind to draw me to their side. Nevertheless, I know the importance of guarding national sovereignty." Charles Bell, who had been a friend

of the 13th Dalai Lama for years, wrote in his *Biography of the 13th Dalai Lama*: "By 1925, the Dalai Lama had become increasingly staunch in bypassing the British to contact the Chinese directly."

The 13th Dalai Lama was very popular with the Tibetan people. Old residents of Lhasa often retell stories about him handed down from their parents and grandparents. According to them, the 13th Dalai Lama was determined to carry out reform, and did a great deal for the betterment of Tibet. But his efforts were obstructed by the oppositions from the three major monasteries. When he was in power, they say, local government decrees were carried out, society was in good order, and officials dared not accept bribes, at least not publicly. However, corruption reappeared and grew rife when Tibet was ruled by a regent later. In order to supervise officials, secular and clerical, the 13th Dalai Lama organized a team of undercover agents to probe official wrongdoing. The residents of Lhasa all knew that the people selling parrots, sparrows or dogs on the Barkor were all the Dalai Lama's "informers." When the informers came to report to him, the Dalai Lama would see them alone on the lawn outside the northern entrance to the Norbu Lingka.

The 13th Dalai Lama was very fond of the gardens of the Norbu Lingka, where he resided during the summer. There, he planted trees and flowers, and raised pet animals. Once, after a ceremony for his return to the Potala Palace on an autumn day, he went straight

The entrance to the Norbu Lingka, the Dalai Lama's summer palace, in the early 20th century. *

Gifts from Qing emperors to Dalai Lamas.

back to the Norbu Lingka quietly. People of Lhasa still remember that flowers such as black rose, silk rose and apple-fragrance rose presented to Central Government delegates by the 14th Dalai Lama were grown by his predecessor in the Norbu Lingka gardens.

The 13th Dalai Lama particularly liked horses and mules, and spent many hours with the ones he housed in two stables he had built in the Norbu Lingka. He even built a Horse-viewing Hall. At his orders, fine horses were selected from all over and sent to the Norbu Lingka. When a good steed arrived, he would go in person to have a look at it. He had all kinds of horses and mules, including renowned Xining horses, tall and robust horses from the West, short and clever Sichuan horses, and mules with fine-colored hide, strong physique and elegant gait. He would give each a name. At the time of his death, he had as many as 710 horses and mules. Apart from hay, more than 20,000 kilograms of beans were needed to feed them each month. The horse shoes they wore were all imported from India. Their

In 1924, the 13th Dalai Lama dismissed Khenpo (Abbot) Losang Tseten of Yonghegong Monastery in Beijing, who had been appointed by him in 1918 as the resident representative of the three monasteries, and appointed Kunchok Jungnas in his place. In reality, the abbot was the representative in Beijing of the 13th Dalai Lama and the Gaxag government. The picture shows a memorial submitted by Kunchok Jungnas to the government of the Republic of China. *

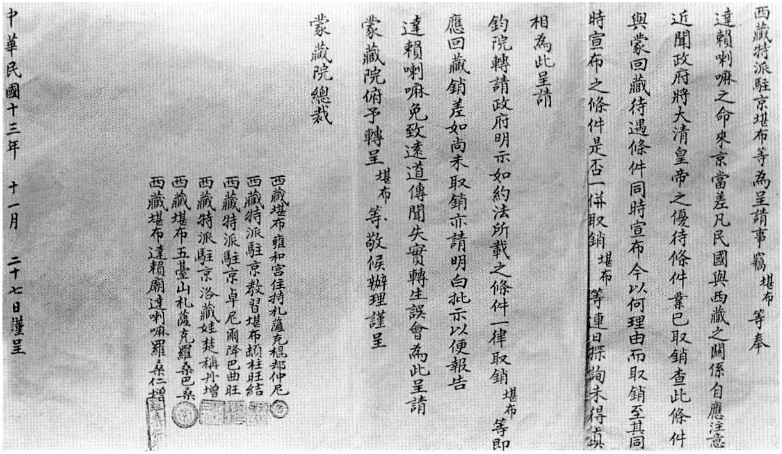

西藏特派駐京堪布等為呈請事竊堪布等奉
達賴喇嘛之命來京當差凡民國與西藏之關係自應注意
近聞政府將大清皇帝之優待條件業已取銷查此條件
與蒙回藏待遇條件同時宣布令以何理由而取銷至其同
時宣布之條件是否一併取銷堪布等連日探詢未得其詳
相為此呈請
鈞院轉請政府明示如約法所載之條件一律取銷堪布等即
應回藏銷差如尚未取銷亦請明白批示以便報告
達賴喇嘛免致達道傳聞失實轉生誤會為此呈請
蒙藏院俯予轉呈堪布等敬候辦理謹呈
蒙藏院總裁

西藏堪布雍和宮住持札薩克楊克郑仲尼
西藏特派駐京教習堪布頡桂旺結
西藏特派駐京卓尼爾降巴曲旺
西藏特派駐京洛藏娃楚稱外增
西藏堪布五臺山札薩克羅色羔
西藏堪布達柏廟達州喇羅桑仁增

中華民國十三年 十一月 二十七日謹呈

Monks perform a religious dance.

saddle cushions were made of yellow woolen fabric. Every day, the 13th Dalai Lama would ride his favorite horse to his office from his residence. In the evenings, he often took a walk leading a horse. After he passed away, the horses and mules were sold to merchants and nobles.

The tragedy of the life of the 13th Dalai Lama lay in the fact that the reforms which he knew Tibet so badly needed ran counter to the interests of the ruling class of monks and nobles. His efforts to bring Tibetan society into the 20th century, were largely neutralized by the conservative forces, to his dismay, and to the detriment of his beloved land and of China as a whole.

Residents in Lhasa are watching a Tibetan opera performance. *

The fifth Reting Hutuktu Thubten Jampel Yeshe served as the regent from 1934 to 1942. *

A photo of Living Buddha Reting taken by the 10th Living Buddha Demo. *

The Final Dirge

The seeds of "Tibetan independence" which Britain had been tending finally began to sprout when Taktra Rimpoche, the regent who ruled Tibet following the death of the 13th Dalai Lama, arrested and executed in 1947 Reting, a patriotic Living Buddha, accusing him of "being too pro-Han" and threw himself into the embrace of Britain.

After World War II ended in 1945, a pro-Han and anti-British feeling began to grow in Tibet. When the Central Government led by the Kuomintang convened the National Assembly to amend the Constitution in Nanjing, the government of Tibet sent a delegation to attend the conference, but in the name of "Thanking the Allies Delegation," to express its gratitude to the Allies and the Nanjing government for their war effort. The act typically reflected the mentality of the ruling

The 13th Dalai Lama with Charles Bell of Britain. The latter worked in Tibet and neighboring regions for more than 20 years, and did a lot of pre-paratory work for Britain's interference in Tibetan affairs. He wrote the *Biography of the 13th Dalai Lama.*

elite of Tibet. It was obviously self-contradictory, and the result naturally turned out to be just the opposite of what was intended.

The delegation first went to India, where it consulted with the British governor of India and the ambassador of the United States to India. The British wrote a letter to the Gaxag government to dissuade it from sending the delegation to Nanjing, and the delegation turned to the Chinese Embassy in India for help. The delegates were warmly welcomed by the embassy officials, who helped them get to Nanjing on time. Though the delegates did not applaud or cast votes as requested by the Gaxag government, their presence in itself indicated that Tibet was part of China. After the assembly, they toured Beijing, Shanghai and other places of interest. It was one year later, in 1947, that the delegation returned to Tibet.

Meanwhile, Britain had persuaded the

The sedan-chair of the Dalai Lama was carried by eight persons. His entourage would hold lines of ropes attached to the vehicle.

Whenever the Dalai Lama left his palace, there would be a long procession accompanying him.

authorities in Tibet to send a delegation to the Asian Relations Conference in New Delhi. The Tibet government complied, and the arrival of the delegation was hailed by the major Indian newspapers. Hugh Richardson, the commercial attaché at the British Embassy in New Delhi, suggested that if the delegation had its own flag it would be claiming to represent an independent country. He wasted no time in notifying the Gaxag.

But Tibet had no national flag, and so the Gaxag sent its army's flag, which showed a lion against a background of snowy peaks.

Another dilemma concerned a national anthem for Tibet. One of the Tibetan delegates sang a song called *The Beauties of the Plum Flower River*, which was then played at the conference. This was originally a song popular in Shanghai in the 1920s to 1930s. Later on, it somehow got into Tibet and was used as the Tibetan army song with new words in praise of the Dalai Lama. Now all of a sudden it served as a "national anthem."

The Indian government, which was soon to shake off the colonial fetters imposed on it by Britain and become independent, inherited the British legacy and secretly supported those who were plotting the "independence" of Tibet. It hoisted the so-called national flag of Tibet together with those of other countries, and hung a map of China which did not include Tibet in the conference hall. A strong protest by China got them removed.

In 1948, the Gaxag government organized a trade

The seat of the Living Buddha Reting was the Reting Monastery in Tanggo Township, Lhünzhub County, very close to the upper reaches of the Lhasa River. The monastery was built some 900 years ago. *

Reting and his men, picture taken by the 10th Living
Buddha Demo in 1935. *

Sharchenchok was the prison of the Potala Palace, in which the Gaxag government held upper-class people. Living Buddha Reting was poisoned here on May 7, 1947. *

mission to visit India, Britain and the United States. The economic objective was to purchase gold or obtain hard currency to back the Tibetan currency, and establish direct trade relations between Tibet and Britain and the United States. Its political task was to win support from big powers to support Tibet's "independence" and membership of the United Nations. But it encountered various handicaps. The first issue was the visa problem, for Tibet had no passports or diplomatic relations with other countries. Finally, the Gaxag issued makeshift passports and the delegation got visas in Hong Kong. The delegation's request for a loan of two million US dollars was rebuffed, and it could get no country to back its claim of "independence" for Tibet.

In 1949, the Gaxag government organized another delegation to the West, hoping to win military support. But even before it had left Tibet, Britain and the United

A grand memorial service was carried out after the passing away of the 13th Dalai Lama.

States indicated that it would not be welcome.

About this time, another Tibetan delegation was waiting to meet representatives of the People's Republic of China in India. The delegation asked Jawaharlal Nehru, the first prime minister of independent India, to mediate between Lhasa and Beijing. Nehru gave a categorical reply

that if Tibet insisted on total independence, agreement would be difficult to reach.

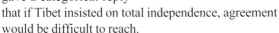

Hugh Richardson, British representative, in front of the Commercial Office in Lhasa. *

By that time, Tibet had been dropped from the list of foreign aid recipients of India and Britain. But suddenly the United States began to show a special interest in Tibet. This was a result of the collapse of the Chiang Kai-shek regime, and the US realized that Tibetan separatists might be used to contain the People's Republic of China.

A sacred Buddhist dance performed in Deyangshar Square in the Potala Palace. * (1957)

Chapter 6
The Fading of
Legendary Figures

   The Potala Palace is comprised of two parts, namely, the White Palace (in the east), started in 1645, and the Red Palace (in the west), started in 1690. The construction took half a century to complete. The picture shows the celebration ceremony for the completion of the Red Palace. *

Half a century has now passed. Descendents of aristocrats, serfs, beggars and singsong girls are all equal in today's Tibetan society. Descendents of aristocrats prefer to have their family name before their own name to indicate that they are somehow different from commoners. But when talking of the past, they ignore it, with a mere smile. Once, when I made some critical comments about a noted figure of the past, one man in the party pointed to another and said that he was the descendent of that person. The guy just smiled, bearing no grudge at all. I have often been to a mountain village named Chagu on the southern bank of the Lhasa River, which used to be a manorial estate of the Drepung Monastery. Once when I was there, I noticed that the villagers were fascinated by the TV drama *Creation of the Gods*, a famous classic of ancient China, dubbed into Tibetan, and watched it every evening. Recently, I heard a story about the people of a village in Tsang writing a letter to the local government demanding dismissal of their village head. The reason was that their neighboring villages were able to watch TV programs but their village was unable to do so. This village was in an area once under the jurisdiction of the Panchen Lama.

The old times, together with their old systems, have gone forever. If the Tibetan people could have a choice, I bet they would prefer to be commoners today than nobles in the old days. The old days, like old photos, are fading. We might make out a few frustrated and indignant faces amidst a group of vague figures. They came to this world at the wrong time, and they had so much to say yet they were unable to make it clear. They groped in darkness with only a candle giving them a slim hope of finding their way forward. At the thought of those people, I want to write something about them to lift the weight from my heart. It might also be a solace to my readers. No matter how depressed a society might be, there is bound to be a struggle against destiny, to gain the light of humanism.

Yum-bu-gla-sgang, the first castle in Tibet, is said to have been built by the first chieftain of the Yalong tribe in the second century. * (1958)

Living Buddha Taktra.

10th Living Buddha Demo

The life of Dainzin Gyatso, the 10th Living Buddha Demo, is fascinating. He came into this world at the turn of the 20th century. Both his parents were from renowned families; his father was from the Ngapoi clan, while his mother was a member of the Langdun clan, of which the 13th Dalai Lama was also a member. Dainzin Gyatso's mother was the 13th Dalai Lama's aunt. Dainzin was chosen to be the reincarnation of the ninth Living Buddha Demo.

However he did not follow the beaten track as arranged by the Providence. Since the decision to strip the title of the ninth Demo and confiscate his property had been confirmed by a decree issued by the Qing Court, all formalities to restore the title had to be carried out in Beijing. But it took two reigns, Emperor

Monks wearing masks are going to perform at a party, the
Dance of the Gods, held in the Potala Palace. * (1957)

Guangxu and Emperor Xuantong, to complete. When the decree arrived in Lhasa, the Qing Dynasty had collapsed.

When the news of the fall of the Qing Dynasty reached Lhasa, the Qing troops stationed in the city mutinied. After the turmoil, they were disarmed, and sent back to the hinterland via the sea route.

The Dance of the Gods held after the ritual to drive out evil spirits in front of the Jokhang Monastery, during the Monlam Prayer Festival in summer. *

As a consequence of the turmoil, Dainzin Gyatso lost everything: the title of the 10th Living Buddha Demo Hutuktu which had been only resumed not long ago, Tengyeling, the Tag-moi Monastery, manorial estates and land in Lhasa, the east Tibet and the south Tibet. Dainzin was then only twelve years old.

Dainzin Gyatso began his religious study and obtained the highest academic degree, Lha-rams-pa (doctor of divinity), at the age of 19. When he was 23, he entered the Lower Tantric House to study Esoteric Buddhism. To concentrate better, he stayed in a cave in the western suburbs of Lhasa. It was there he happened to meet a Nepalese photographer. Ever since then, his life took an abrupt turn, and he headed for a new world alone.

The 13th Dalai Lama thought highly of this cousin of his for

On September 1, 1934, Regent Reting met Huang Musong, emissary of the government of the Republic of China. Living Buddha Demo was invited to take photographs on the occasion.

his cleverness and talent, and was disappointed when he embarked on a photographic career. In the summer of the year when he died, he called Dainzin Gyatso to the Norbu Lingka, and told him that he had meant to appoint him to be Ga-Idan-khri-pa, a lofty religious position. "But you seem to have no heart for anything like that," he sighed. "You have got to look after yourself in future."

Perhaps due to the bitter experiences of his childhood, Dainzin Gyatso seemed to have seen through the essence of the political and religious life of the Tibetan elite. As a result, he kept politics at arm's length, almost by instinct. The camera brought him a new artistic vista. He put all his enthusiasm and attention into the lens, from which he could see a real as well as a surreal world. All his joy and all his distress were rooted in the black-and-white pictures he took. The dark room was his haven. Political rivalry, the ups and downs of official life and racking one's brains to make more money were things remote from him.

Living Buddha Reting and Dainzin Gyatso were on good term. The photo of Reting taken by Dainzin Gyatso has been printed and seen by hundreds of thousands of people. When Reting acted as the regent, he returned the Tag-moi Monastery in Nyingchi and some manorial estates to Dainzin Gyatso. When Reting had to give up the regency under pressure, the first choice he though of to succeed him was Dainzin Gyatso. Of course, the latter turned the offer down. Then Radregn turned to Living Buddha Pabungka, who also refused the post. Then he asked Living Buddha Taktra Rimpoche, who was already in his 70s, to assume the regency on condition that Taktra would return the position to him three years later. This was a fatal mistake.

If only Dainzin Gyatso had become the regent, the

The Sakya Monastery was the center of political and religious power 600 years ago. The picture shows a scene from the Dance of the Guardian Deities on the Celestial Burial Ground performed by monks on the occasion of the Monlam Prayer Festival in summer. (Photo by Zhang Ying)

history of Tibet would have gone in another direction. In 1938, he, now the 10th Living Buddha Demo, married and bought two manorial estates. Besides, he also bought a Carbine camera from India. Not only did he himself refuse to return to the ranks of the Ti-

Tibetan soldiers in ancient uniform. * (1957)

betan elite, he prevented his son, my old colleague Bangphyug Dorje, from becoming a Living Buddha.

One day in the 1950s, a man came to see Dainzin Gyatso and cheerfully told him that his house had appeared in the Magic Lake, one of the signs indicating the reincarnation of a Living Buddha. He said that this meant that his second son was such a reincarnation. Dainzin Gyatso sent the man packing. It was only the day before he died that he told his son about this.

The mansion of the King of Shannan. * (1961)

People dressed up like ancient warriors during the Monlam Prayer Festival. *

People dressed up like ancient warriors. * (1957)

Thubten Gonghpel
in Kalimpong, India,
(picture taken some
time between 1937 and
1946).

Thubten Gongphel

I had come across accounts of Thubten Gongphel,
but had never paid much attention to him until I saw an
illustration of him in *The Demise of the Lamaist State.*
Unlike the flaccid, lethargic images of aristocrats in the
other illustrations in that book, he looked slim and tall,
with a serene face. According to the author, the first
half of his life was legendary. I wondered what role he
would play later. It was a few days later I found some
old documents that revealed more information about
him. I learned that his wife was still alive and, what's
more, she was an aunt of a friend of mine.

Thubten Gongphel was born into a serf's family in
Nyemo. He managed to get a job as a gardener in the
Norbu Lingka. There, he also copied sutras. The 13th
Dalai Lama was very fond of him, and made him a
bodyguard. After that, he rose quickly. Power and

wealth grew side by side. He enjoyed more privileges than high-ranking officials in the palace. The Dalai Lama put him in charge of all important work such as the building of a power plant and a mint, and the renovation of the Potala Palace and the Norbu Lingka. What's more significant was that he was asked to form a guard corps with influence and remuneration superior to that of the Tibetan army, or even the Lhasa garrison. He chose its members personally from well-off families, and the corps was equipped with the best weapons of the time. Even parts of its uniforms were ordered from abroad. The epaulettes and cap insignias were made of gold. No one could doubt that this corps was under the direct control of the Dalai Lama, and Thubten Gongphel was the commander.

Leaders of the Tibet Improvement Party (from left: Ponda Rabga, Thubten Gongphel and Changlochen).

Tubdain rode in the Dalai Lama's own Austin motor car to inspect the Norbu Lingka gardens and the corps. Wherever he went, he was greeted by lines of people and saluting army officers. He would wave his hand in casual reply. Though he was now near the peak of power in Tibet, he had no official title. At that time, people addressed him as "Ta Lama," followed by his name. This unofficial title was bestowed on him by the Dalai Lame for his good performance in repairing the Pobrang Palace in the Norbu Lingka. All this did not go unnoticed by the agents of Britain in Lhasa, who saw in him a future power center.

Despite his power and influence, there seems to

be no record of any corruption or irregularity connected with Tubdain. Most of what has been written about him praises his magnanimity and wisdom. Nevertheless, shortly after the 13th Dalai Lama passed away, Tubdain was accused of murdering him, even though everyone, even his political enemies, knew clearly that he would not have benefited from the death of the Dalai Lama. He was first detained, and then sent in exile, along with his father. The property of both him and his relatives was confiscated. To add insult to injury, father and son were expelled on the 29th day of the 12th month by the Tibetan calendar, a day for sending off "ghosts."

In the two months from the death of the 13th Dalai Lama to his expulsion from Lhasa, Tubdain had plenty of opportunity to either seize power and save himself, using his guard corps, or escape with the help of powerful friends. But he did neither — evidence that he was not politically ambitious.

The Lotus Pavilion in the Norbu Lingka. *
(1957).

The place of exile for his father was Nyemo, his hometown. Stripped of all their property, the clan became serfs once more. The 28-year-old Thubten Gongphel was sent into exile in the area of Gongbo. There, this first victim of the fierce political strife after the death of the 13th Dalai Lama, spent three years in exile. Realizing that return to Lhasa was hopeless, he, together with Changlochen, an exiled poet, crossed the Himalayas to Kalimpong in India. There he met Ponda Rabga, a mem-

Mask and costume
of a dancer of the
Dance of the Gods. *
(1957)

ber of the Ponda clan, and Gedun Chophel, a scholar studying in India. The four Tibetan intellectuals planned a move which shook British India and Tibet. Thus Thubten Gongphel embarked on the second period of his life.

For a period of 10 years, he simply disappeared. Then, he was expelled from India for sending evidence to the Gaxag government that Moindawang was illegally occupied by British India. The corrupt Gaxag government, however, was under the influence of the British, and betrayed Tubdain and his companions to the British authorities in India.

It is recorded in documents kept in the Archives of the Ministry of Internal Affairs of India that there

The party emblem of the Tibet Improvement Party.

existed a party known as the Tibet Improvement Party (Nub-legs-bcos-skyid-sdug), also known as the Tibet Revolutionary Party. The establishment of this political party was initiated in 1939 by Ponda Rabga, who once served on the Commission for Mongolian and Tibetan Affairs of the Republic of China. Ponda Rabga, Changlochen and Thubten Gongphel became the leaders of the party. The Tibet Improvement Party had insignia and a program. It printed several thousand application forms. This party expressly advocated the freeing of Tibet from its present totalitarian government, the carrying out of revolutionary reforms and the rebuilding of the political and social systems of Tibet, that is, the founding of a democratic republic. We know little about its activities or how many members it had. All we have are some photos showing a few young men who look much more dignified than ordinary Tibetan people at that time. One thing is certain, and that is that Thubten Gongphel had transformed himself from a servant of the theocracy into a revolutionary who was determined to overthrow the old system.

None of these people have left any writings about their activities. We have no idea what was on the mind of Thubten Gongphel. How could he make such a drastic change? How did he fit into an environment which was entirely different from that of the old society? How did he complete his mental transformation from one extreme to another? His last dozen years, or the third period of his life, indicate the infinite possibilities for a man.

The British and the Indian governments, together

with the Gaxag government, nipped this party in the bud. Diplomats of the Republic of China stationed in New Delhi informed them of the imminent danger, and a large number of documents and files of the party members were quickly destroyed. When Thubten Gongphel was expelled from India, he claimed to be a citizen of the Republic of China, and he flew to Nanjing under the protection of the Chinese Embassy in India.

Thubten Gongphel returned to Lhasa in 1947. Again, we have no idea if he had any special mission. What we know is that he set up his own business. When the People's Liberation Army (PLA) arrived in Lhasa in October 1951, we saw his tall figure and cheerful expression amidst the crowds of people who had turned out to welcome the PLA. Soon he became a cadre, and was engaged in purchasing grain for the PLA and transporting timber for the headquarters of the Tibet Military Region. In 1954, at the age of 49, he got married and started a happy family. Two years later, the Preparatory Committee of the Tibet Autonomous Region was established. Thubten Gongphel was appointed Deputy Director-General of the Geology Bureau. He led exploration teams and prospected for mineral re-

A pilgrim on Barkor Street. * (1956)

Monk and lay officials on their way to attend the Monlam Prayer Festival in Lhasa. *

The Samyas Monastery. *

sources all over Tibet. He participated in the celebrations in Beijing for National Day, 1957. There, he met Chairman Mao, Liu Shaoqi, Zhou Enlai....

The year 1959 saw the Democratic Reform carried out in Tibet. After that, Thubten Gongphel was appointed deputy head of the Administrative Division of the General Office of the Preparatory Committee of the Tibet Autonomous Region. He was in charge of production development and logistics. In those early days, there was a serious shortage of goods. He opened up a farm and a cattle ranch for the Preparatory Committee. Never flagging in his diligence and devotion to his tasks, Tubdain fell ill from prolonged overwork, and in December 1963 he died of cerebral hemorrhage at the age of 58.

A man dressed as a warrior. * (1956)

A scene of the Monlam Prayer Festival held on the 5th day of the 5th month by the Tibetan calendar in Lhasa. *

A flower made of butter. *

Gedun Chophel

Though clad in a kasaya (a patchwork outer vestment worn by a lama) all his life, Gedun Chophel (1903-1951) was never fettered by convention, and began seeking truth when he was a boy.

Gedun Chophel was born into a noted family of the Ning-ma Sect (Ancient Mystic Order) in Qinghai Province. He was chosen as the "soul boy" reincarnation of a Living Buddha by the monastery of the Ning-ma Sect, and instructed in the doctrines of the sect in his childhood. At the age of 17, he went to Labrang Monastery, in Gannan, to study, staying there for seven years. A very clever and talented man, he began to doubt what he had been taught. Unorthodox thoughts grew in his mind day by day. He challenged the classic syllabus of the monastery, and was driven out. He continued his studies in the Drepung Monastery for another seven years.

In Lhasa, he became known for his profound understanding of Buddhism. He was also an expert in the Five Luminaries (phonology, technology, Buddhism, logic and medicine), as

Gedun Chophel in India (center).

well as in sutra debating, poetry, painting and writing. He earned a living by painting portraits of the Buddha for well-off families in the city. This also materially prepared him for his future travels. His reputation for being unconventional also grew.

In 1934, when he was 34 years old, he gave up the opportunity to take an examination for the qualification of Lha-rams-pa, the highest degree among lamaist Doctors of Divinity, and left Tibet, together with an Indian scholar, to see more of the world. It was 12 years before he returned.

Gedun Chophel went to India, Nepal, Bengal and Sri Lanka to study Buddhism in Buddhist holy cities, as well as local customs, nature, geography and histories of nationalities. Apart from his mastery of the ancient Tibetan language, he also assiduously studied English and Sanskrit. He wrote many thought-provoking articles, which are still of academic value today. In particular, he learned the advanced scientific knowledge of that time. We also know that he was one of the founders of the Tibet Improvement Party. We have learned from some studies about him in foreign countries that during his stay in India, he was engrossed in the study of the political philosophy and theory of colonialism of Karl Marx. He gradually came to realize the necessity of carrying out a great reform or even revolution in Tibet. He advocated the abolition of the feudal system and the barring of monks from trade and land-owning. He advocated land reform, legal system reform and democratic politics.

When Gedun Chophel returned to Lhasa, in 1946, he was a man with high aspirations and brand-new ideas. He had already secretly traveled for a month to the area of Tibet occupied by the British authorities in India, behind the so-called McMahon line and drew a map. For almost two and half years after his return to Lhasa he was held in prison; then for another three years he was under house arrest. He died of illness just after seeing the liberation of Tibet. This intelligent man with progressive ideas and aspirations was lost in a sea of darkness and stupidity.

The Treasure Display Party is held annually in Lhasa. People play all kinds of musical instruments, which are said to have been introduced to Tibet by Princess Wen-cheng. * (1957)

Mani Stones. *

Luckily he had just completed his work, *Travels in Various Countries*. This book is highly critical of ancient Tibet and ancient India from the perspectives of culture and religion. It traces the origin of authentic spiritual pursuit, and ferrets out falsehoods. It expounds the truth, and refutes superstition. He says at the beginning of the book: "I have renounced speculation, renounced the practice of cooking up far-fetched tales in order to win popularity, renounced acts of currying favor with others and thereby not having the courage to tell the truth, and renounced the surrendering of judgment of right or wrong in exchange for fame and fortune."

He sharply criticized the phenomena in Tibetan tradition of the blind worship of India and the belittling of Tibet. He expressed his indignation at barbarous Hindu practices and caste system, raising doubts about

Each area and each monastery in Tibet has its own religious festivals. In the seventh month by the Tibetan calendar, the Tashilhunpo Monastery holds the Shikmo-chenpo Festival, which is the largest festival in Xigaze. The performance of the Vajra Deity Dance performed by monks lasts for three days. (Photo by Zhang Ying)

the Buddhist outlook.

Is the earth round or flat? He wrote an essay on that too, and it was published in a journal named the *Mirror* in India. Today, even children know the answer. But half a century ago in Tibet, it was an outrageous question. Any Tibetan who dared to claim that the earth was round had to have the courage of Galileo in those days.

Gedun Chophel was not only an expert in religion, but also in poetry, art, languages, history, geography, local customs, archeology and Ti-

Adding butter to a huge Buddhist lamp. * (1958)

betan medicine. He even studied sexology. His work *Desire* shook Tibetan society. All his works and essays reflected his advanced thinking.

Though equipped with evolution, humanism and Marxism, essentially he was a Buddhist. But he cast away the traditional approach to study, and adopted a new approach that was close to that of modern times. In his mind, Buddhism was a philosophy which must not be followed blindly, so as to exclude superstition.

For a thousand years, he was the only one who upheld humanism and human rights in a society supposedly ruled by "divine power." He left Tibet and saw much of the world. He detected the defects in religion and language at their origin, and cleared up mysteries. He met the poet Rabindranath Tagore and many other men of letters and philosophy. Guided by their thoughts, he blazed a new trail of rationality.

Sorcerers at the Shabten Gompa Monastery in Nagqu Township hold an exorcism session. * (1956)

Gedun Chophel was jailed by the Taktra Rimpoche regime and the British conspirators, not for his ideas or his involvement in the Tibet Improvement Party, but on a trumped up charge of forging banknotes.

The Tibet Improvement Party, with its headquarters in Kalimpong, was banned. Gedun Chophel was frustrated, for he could see no ray of hope. Though he still wrote poems, he ended up an alcoholic.

In 1949, when he was finally freed, he was incurably ill. When the advance troops of the PLA entered Lhasa in 1951, Zhang Jingwu, representative of the Central People's Government, sent doctors to give Gedun Chophel treatment, but unfortunately it was too late.

An entire half a century has passed since then, and many important events have taken place in this period. Tibet has been changing and progressing. The reforms which Gedun Chophel advocated have now been realized. His works have been collected and published, and some have been translated. *The Best of the Selected Works of Gedun Chophel* has been published in Chinese. Many Tibetologists, both Chinese and foreign, have been studying this important Tibetan figure. Dr. Du Yongbin has published *A Miraculous Lama of 20th Century – A Critical Biography of Master Gedun Chophel, Pioneer of Humanism.* Gedun Chophel's lofty ideas, as contained in his works, are still valid some half a century later, and of special significance not only for Tibet today.

Old Lhasa is now a part of history, but I feel that stories about old Lhasa and its fascinating figures should be handed down from generation to generation.

People pray for a good harvest, and offer barley wine and food items on the first morning after the ceremony for the beginning of Spring Plowing. *

Upper-class monks in front of the Jokhang Monastery ready to
attend the annul Monlam Prayer Festival. * (1957)

Editors' Note

Old Lhasa · A Sacred City at Dusk is the latest in our "Old City" series presenting through text and photographs a unique view of the history of China through a focus on the development of several of its most important cities. Earlier books in the series include: *Old Beijing, Old Shanghai, Old Xi'an,* and *Old Nanjing.*

For each "Old City" book, a prominent local writer was commissioned to provide in-depth knowledge as well as to give local flavor to the writing. The richness of the text is embellished by a generous display of historic photographs that illustrate the always-changing city landscape, from life in the streets to life in the corridors of power. The combined result is an intimate look at China not readily available elsewhere.

In publishing this series, we have been guided by the hope that our efforts will provide a new perspective on Chinese urban history, culture, architecture, planning and development that will enhance our readers' understanding of China as a whole.

Originally published in Chinese by the Jiangsu Fine Arts Publishing House, the "Old City" series in its English edition is published jointly by the Foreign Languages Press and the Jiangsu Fine Arts Publishing House.

Foreign Languages Press
October 2002, Beijing

图书在版编目（CIP）数据

老拉萨：圣城暮色/马丽华著.－北京：外文出版社，2002.10
（老城市系列）
ISBN 7–119–03124–4

Ⅰ．老… Ⅱ．马… Ⅲ．拉萨市－地方史－史料－英文Ⅳ.K297.51

中国版本图书馆 CIP 数据核字（2002）第 061742 号

中文原版

> 选题策划　叶兆言　何兆兴　顾华明　速　加
> 主　　编　朱成梁
> 副 主 编　顾华明　何兆兴　马振犊
> 著　　文　马丽华
> 图片供稿　中国第二历史档案馆　陈宗烈
> 装帧设计　顾华明
> 责任编辑　顾华明

英文版

> 策划编辑　兰佩瑾
> 翻　　译　王明杰
> 英文编辑　郁　苓
> 责任编辑　兰佩瑾

老拉萨·圣城暮色

ⓒ 外文出版社
外文出版社出版
（中国北京百万庄大街 24 号）
邮政编码 100037
外文出版社网址：http://www.flp.com.cn
外文出版社电子信箱：info@flp.com.cn
　　　　　　　　 sales@flp.com.cn
利丰雅高制作（深圳）有限公司印刷
2003 年(大 32 开)第 1 版
2003 年第 1 版第 1 次印刷
（英文）
ISBN 7–119–03124–4/J · 1615(外)
08000（精）

OLD CITY